D0863124

Who am I?

the seeker's guide to nowhere

Esther Veltheim

PUBLISHED BY PARAMA

Also by Esther Veltheim
  Beyond Concepts - The investigation of who you are not
  PUBLISHED BY PARAMA
Also by Esther & John Veltheim
  Reiki - the Science, Metaphysics, and Philosophy
  PUBLISHED BY PARAMA

First published in April 2001
by
PaRama INC.
5500 Bee Ridge Drive, #103
Sarasota, FL 34233, USA

© Esther Veltheim
All rights reserved.

ISBN   1-929762-02-x

Printed in the USA

e-mail: parama@home.com
Web site: www.parama.com

Cover design by Lorin H. Sourbeck

Preface

As a tiny child I remember time and again saying to my mother, "It's okay Mummy, I know I am an orphan, you can tell me. It won't upset me." My mother had no idea how I had come upon the notion that I was an adoptive child because this certainly wasn't the case.

For my part, it wasn't that I disliked my parents. On the contrary, it was just that I couldn't reconcile myself with their perception of me. In face of this dilemma the only solution I could come up with was that I wasn't the person they were trying to make me believe I was.

As the years passed, like everyone else, I accumulated and sometimes discarded various identities. The trouble was that the identities that suited me didn't seem to suit anyone else. And the ones I adopted to suit others didn't suit me. This is a battle that you might be quite familiar with yourself, especially if you have a rebellious nature.

It was only in my late thirties, when all my identities came crashing down around my ears, that I began to question their meaning. "Is this all life is about, 'becoming this or that'?" I was sure there had to be *more* to life, and to me, than I was aware of. I had no idea that my subsequent search for Self would reveal that "I" was far, far *less* than I had spent my life believing.

You may be thinking, "That's hardly a conclusion I have any desire to come to." But think back to when you were a tiny child, minus all the well-honed identities you have now. In those days life was experienced fully and uninhibitedly. It was only when you began believing you had to *become* other than you were that you started losing sight of the sense of freedom you had as a child.

The person you *think* you are is rather like a jigsaw puzzle that you have been adding pieces to all your life. This book is not about to give you more pieces to add to the puzzle. It is about helping you to understand that this "jigsaw puzzle" you call "me" is a false representation of You, which means it is NOT You.

When the illusory "you" is fully recognized for what it is—a faulty perception—this relative change is what is referred to as *enlightenment*. And do note that *enlightenment* only describes a relative change, nothing real. Contrary to many peoples' connotations of this word, *enlightenment* does not mean that "you" suddenly remember who You really are. It is helpful that you understand this at the outset of reading, because this book certainly isn't about "attaining" enlightenment.

If this is your first introduction to the subject of ontology—the investigation of being—you may do well to begin by reading my first book *Beyond Concepts—The investigation of who you are not*.

The word *mind* not only denotes *memory*—the accumulation of thoughts—but also *forgetfulness*—the absence of clear thoughts. Who or what You Really are has nothing to do with either remembering or forgetting. *You* have never undergone any change, have never forgotten, and don't need to remember Your Self.

In the initial stages of its formation, the mind is a fairly clear reflector of You. This is because thoughts do not yet describe You as an object. With the onset of interaction with the world, the mind reflects your previously wordless sense of self in the words "I am." The mind then links the body to this knowing and the thought "I am some-body" is the mental distortion that results.

When you start re-evaluating your sense of self sincerely, this is when you "become" what is called *a seeker*. The more one-pointed your yearning to know Self, the more intense seeking becomes. This intensity and one-pointed focus gradually disrupts all the beliefs you have accumulated about yourself. If this disruption is powerful enough, it leads to the total conviction: "I can never know or understand Self." Only when this understanding becomes a total conviction does the mind stop booting up distorted information about You.

Enlightenment denotes the full realization that who you *think* you are is a faulty perception. This is why, contrary to common belief, no "one" ever *attains* enlightenment. *Enlightenment* is just a concept that describes a relative change in perception.

The written teachings of Sri Ramana Maharshi, Sri Nisargadatta Maharaj, and other great sages paved the way for my understanding of these dynamics. Without them, the question "who am I?" may well have remained no more than a frustrated sigh upon my lips.

My subsequent brief encounter with Ramesh Balsekar shed intense *light* on the intellectual understanding I had of Self. In that instant, the misperception of Self began to subside.

Brief encounters and correspondences with my second teacher, Wendell Henckel, helped to further dispel mental conditioning.

Were it not for these great teachers and the foundations of intellectual understanding they gave me, this book might never have been written. Its subject matter is paradoxical because it concerns That which is unexplainable and cannot be put into words. However, from my own experience, the more directly the Truth can be pointed to, the greater the potential for the mind to lose its distortions. These distortions—the thoughts "I am somebody," "I am this and that"—are what keep you ignorant of Self.

It isn't that I made a conscious decision to disseminate pointers in a book. The following writings simply emerged spontaneously over the period of ten days while I holed up in a little apartment away from home.

I am especially grateful to my husband, John, for his boundless enthusiasm and encouragement. Daily he would visit me, bringing supplies in an effort to get me to eat and take breaks. But his patient urgings were no match for what I can only call the obsession of writing. Little eating or sleeping was possible until it was done.

How Ramesh wrote all his books by hand I have no idea. I had the good fortune to be privy to a computer; otherwise, I can't imagine how my hands could have kept up with flow of words.

The following pages contain no absolute truth, because That which You are cannot be verbalized. However, these writings may afford you a sign-post which will point you *away* from who you *think* you are, *towards* the Truth. Between the words and beyond concepts, You already are.

This means that as a so-called seeker you are not searching for some-thing that is missing. You have no-where to aim for because You *are* the destination. Hence the sub-title, *The seeker's guide to nowhere.*

You'll find a fair amount of repetition, particularly in the second and third chapters. This isn't because I am trying to brain-wash you with my ideas. On the contrary, repetition is used as a means of jarring you out of your intellectual comfort-zone so that you can begin using your own power of discrimination constructively.

Who You really are is not a mystery unto it-Self, but before this is *realized* there must be total commitment to the solving of what appears to be the ultimate riddle. When nothing else matters but the search for Self, the intensity of this yearning dispels all other desires. When this happens, the fire of yearning takes over and does all the work.

Esther Veltheim
August 4, 2000

*You want peace so badly and in the wanting of it there is no peace.
Only when the wanting stops will you discover that peace has been there all along.*
EV

Contents

Preface   **3**

Self-Enquiry   **9**

Existence   **15**

Who am I?   **23**

Essential Nature and True Nature   **45**

God and Religion   **61**

Enlightenment and other Misconceptions   **83**

Control and Purpose   **101**

Consciousness and the Mind   **121**

Thoughts and Thinking   **139**

Censorship, Reasons, and Synchronicity   **159**

The Process of Enlightenment   **171**

The Frustrated Seeker   **187**

Self-Realization - the Paradox   **217**

Have pity on those ignorant ones
Who are not on any "path."
Intensify your struggle for
Peace and enlightenment.
Once you are truly purified,
And highly spiritual,
You can place this glowing
Ember of success
Upon the alter of
The ego.
Then come, and sit down beside me,
And rest a while.

Now, tell me.......
Who **are** you?

EV

Self-Enquiry

Sri Ramana Maharshi's teachings of self-enquiry came my way at a time when my reading capacity was very limited. In the previous year my system had sustained severe neuro-toxic poisoning. Among a myriad of symptoms the most devastating was the loss of visual and mental focus. However, the little I was able to read of Ramana's teachings triggered the first stages of conscious seeking.

A couple of years later I met my teacher Wendell. His background is Vedantic, a philosophy that I remain fairly unschooled in to this day. It's mapping of the relative stages of enlightenment did, however, serve as very helpful pointers in the coming years.

The first lesson I remember Wendell teaching me was an exercise in self-enquiry. He asked me to close my eyes and to pose the question, "Who am I?" Intellectually, I already understood that I was not the bodymind or any other object. But, in doing the exercise various answers still came to mind, such as "I don't know," or "I just experience emptiness."

With the arising of each response Wendell pointed out, "You can perceive this concept. In order to perceive anything you must be separate to it. Now go behind it and ask the question again."

For a while thoughts continued to arise, but then nothing came to mind at all. Retrospectively I realized there was tremendous peace when this happened. It was the first time I began to realize that it was impossible to understand Self via the mind.

Because the mind IS concepts, thinking or the perceiving of thoughts has to happen from the perspective of something other than the mind. Thoughts cannot *think* or experience themselves. The mind cannot *think* or experience itself. Such a capacity would be similar to water drinking itself or fire burning itself, which is clearly impossible.

9

Although this dynamic is obvious to me now, when I first met with Wendell I was still strongly identified with the mind. It took a while before the implications of Wendell's exercise really "hit home." At first the idea that one had to be separate to something in order to perceive it helped me to better grasp the idea that I was not the body or any other label. The mind was a different matter.

Intellectually I understood that Self was "beyond understanding," but as a so-called seeker I resembled most seekers. I believed that what I sought was discoverable via the mind. Even though many seekers go to great lengths to still the mind, it is their identification with this concept that fuels the desire be rid of thoughts. If they understood that to perceive the mind "they" have to be separate to it, they would no longer consider it an obstacle.

What I called "me" was an appearance that came about when thoughts linked the sense of presence or "I am" to objects. "I am some-body" was the belief that resulted. Although this person had many aliases—woman, traveler, free-spirit, etc.—the primary identity or the one I fixated most on was the *mind.*

I had always devoured books and all sources of new information. Having left school at the age of fifteen, I considered my minimal education an impediment. As a result I believed I was never intellectually "good enough."

When my body was hit by neuro-toxic poisoning, intellectual focus was severely impaired. To give you an idea of the severity of this, I barely knew my own name. Someone would say something to me and instantaneously I'd forget what had been said. I would say something, or think something, and immediately forget what it was. As you can imagine, this was a severe blow to my primary identity—as critical of that identity as I was.

Clearly, if anyone IS the mind, they are in constant jeopardy. Alzheimer's, senility, and numerous diseases of mental impairment strike people "out of the blue" every day. There I was with an ailment that resembled any one of these and, as befuddled as my thinking was, I began questioning my identity.

For seven or eight years I struggled with the seeming limitations imposed on me. Now I can only think of the poisoning as a gift in that its limitations offered me only two options. Either I could give up and resign myself to depression and struggle, or I could look seriously at the implications of my experience. I chose the latter course of action even though many times I sincerely thought I was going mad in doing so.

At first my questions arose out of sheer frustration, which simply grew. Frustration then turned into resignation and back into frustration again. When I found Ramana's teachings on self-enquiry I was both elated and relieved. Until that point I had berated myself for asking such a ridiculous question as "Who am I?" It seemed to me nothing more than a thought that depressives would come up with. To actually find someone advocating the asking of this question was quite mind-blowing to me.

After meeting Wendell my investigation of self turned into an obsession. It was all I could think about and talk about. Not only did I seem to be driving myself crazy but everyone around me. Fortunately my husband, John, was also a student of Wendell. But, his seeking certainly took a more moderate form than mine. In this way he provided both a patient sounding board and a partner in seeking.

Gradually I began investigating concepts and unraveling them. It became increasingly clear that everything is paradox and that no concept can exist without its opposite in potential within it. I began to realize that thought processes were circular in nature and that it was impossible for my mind to come up with one single concept that was an *absolute* unto itself.

One day, embroiled in my investigation of concepts, I realized that the use of the interrogative pronoun *who* in asking "*Who* am I?" necessarily conjured up the idea of an object-identity. I saw great value in Ramana's process of self-enquiry in that it certainly tripped my thinking processes up. But by this time it had become clear to me that all familiar terminology held the risk of lulling me into habitual thinking processes. This led me to look for another way of questioning my identity. It was then that I began asking, "How is the experiencing of *anything* possible?" and "How do I know that I am?"

By this time my capacity to read had improved somewhat and I began reading the transcripts of Sri Nisargadatta Maharaj's teachings. Therein I found that he frequently asked his disciples these very same questions. The unfamiliarity of these questions served to deepen my understanding that the mind contains absolutely no data on the Truth.

Perhaps my own relative process took a more complex turn than that of most seekers. Certainly the way in which I undertook the investigation of concepts is not considered the easiest "path." But it is considered the most direct of all "paths." This is because other spiritual disciplines risk giving the practitioner of them the idea that they are making progress. In this way, instead of doing something that helps them recognize their distorted perception of the ego, they risk puffing these distortions up even more than before. This clearly defeats the whole object of any spiritual practice.

Jnana yoga—the investigation of concepts—holds no such risk. This is because jnana yoga is not about "personal growth" or evolution. It is the process of "personal dissolution" and involution.

Although the following chapters are written clearly and simply, the reading of them may seem daunting at first. If you have difficulty or find yourself struggling, don't fall into the trap of thinking, "This is too complex." Recognize that it is the unfamiliarity of these lines of thinking that is daunting to you.

Lateral thinking is always a challenge to familiar, comfortable thought processes. But this is precisely why jnana yoga is the most direct method of uprooting you from your comfort zone. As long as you remain in the comfort-zone of familiar thoughts it is very difficult to even begin to understand that who you *think* you are is a faulty perception—an illusion.

If during the reading of this you can set aside rigid ideas and agendas you will find the going much easier. This is not to say, "Don't question what you read." No truths are contained in this book, but all personal "truths" are put into question. It is not a matter of accepting these writings at face value. But the constructive reading and questioning of what is written here can only happen if you first set aside everything you now consider to be true about yourself and life.

Ramesh Balsekar coined the terms "thinking mind" and "working mind" to differentiate between censored, efforted thinking and practical thinking. When enlightenment *happens,* efforted or censored thinking gives way to practical thinking. Thoughts arise and subside with equal ease and the knowing that thoughts are impersonal dispels the *need* to censor any thoughts. In this way thinking is effortless and therefore practical. This describes the "working mind."

A while ago a gentleman who was listening to me talk exclaimed: "You're using lateral logic! I could never have come to this conclusion myself, but what you say now makes total sense to me. I can't believe I didn't see it that way before. But I haven't the foggiest idea how you arrived at this conclusion!"

The following chapters are best described by drawing on this gentleman's coinage of the term "lateral logic." This is because they are written from the perspective of the "working mind." Nothing in this book is written from the standpoint of a personal agenda or any dogma.

People often ask me why I write if I don't have a personal agenda such as the desire to communicate. In part my answer is that writing, and all functioning, happens despite me. This means that there is no particular *reason* behind anything I do. There is pleasure in the idea that benefit may be had from reading what I write. But there is absolutely no *desire* for these writings to be read or appreciated in any particular way.

The second part to my answer would be that enlightenment describes a *relative,* ongoing process. The relative stages of enlightenment are best described as an ongoing involution of focus.

Once the primary misconception of being "some-body" subsides, there is an ongoing subsidence of habitual thought processes. The rigid mind-set, that once veiled the Heart, gives way to an ever-deepening neutrality or peace. This is reflected in the mind in increased clarity of thought. In my case, writing appears to facilitate the mind's involution process.

So, in the reading of this, to some degree or another, you are also engaged in the process of enlightenment—the un-veiling or un-covering of the Heart. You will never find the Truth in any book because the Truth is beyond concepts and so cannot be put into words. The following writings serve only as an expose on the personal lie you call "me." This is perhaps the only truth you will find here, that who you *think* you are does not exist.

You say you are *some-body*
Intelligent and that
You have willpower.
But I ask you,
Can a flame burn itself?
Can water drink itself?
Yes, these are crazy questions.
But *my mind is insane*,
And cannot explain
The world.
All I know is that, "I Am."
Nothing else matters
To Me.

EV

Existence

Of all the pieces of information you have accumulated in your lifetime, there is only one thing you know for certain. You have never needed anyone to teach you about it, and you have never needed anyone to affirm it to you. This conviction is one you have had since you were a tiny child and it is that you exist.

Because the knowing "I am" contains absolutely no doubts, it wouldn't matter how much someone argued with you that you don't exist. You wouldn't feel the need to justify yourself to them, and you wouldn't feel the need to lash out in indignation. This is because *reactionary behavior only happens when beliefs are underlain by doubt.*

Conversely, if someone told you, "You could look better; you should act more appropriately; you should demonstrate more intelligence," these are comments that might well detonate a lot of "buttons" in you.

The reactionary behavior of justifying yourself to others is an indication of two things. One is that the deep knowing "I exist" has been linked to the learned information "I am *some-body*" with a gender, a name, specific roles, and personal volition. The other is that the learned information, "I am some-body," is underlain by doubts.

As soon as you learned "I exist *as some-body*," ambition, desire, and the need to prove yourself was set in motion. In short, what you have learned about yourself has given rise to reactionary behavior, and reactionary behavior is always underlain by doubt.

This means that the more dogmatic your *shoulds* and *should nots* are, ("I should look like this;" "I should be more intelligent;" "I shouldn't act like that," etc.) the more deeply you doubt yourself.

If you understand this, it isn't difficult to see that who you have been taught, and now believe you are, is an identity that has brought you nothing but confusion and struggle.

The body is constantly changing; the mind constantly changing; and your roles are constantly changing. You have learned that you are the sum of these concepts, and as they are always in constant flux, the need to define yourself never ceases. No wonder you are a slave to the desire to control!

When the desire to break free of the desire for control happens, it is time to investigate the beliefs that have brought this struggle about. With a little clear thinking it doesn't take much to recognize that IF control were real and you had it, it isn't something you could ever lose. This is because IF you had control you would have the control to maintain it.

Until now you may have thought in terms of partial control or temporary control. If you had partial control over a raging bull, would you say you have real control? If you had temporary control over your finances, would you say you had real control? The answer is surely "no," and this is because the word *control* describes an absolute.

If you have ever thought you had absolute control but still felt the need to maintain it, this tells you it has *not* been absolute. For why would you need to maintain an absolute?

This simple process of deduction tells you that *there is no such thing as control.*

This same exercise can be done with concepts such as freedom, peace, security, and any other concepts you yearn after. With a little clear thinking you will discover that none of these concepts are absolutes.

You can only know about the concept of freedom because you've been taught about limitation. You have been taught about struggle and that's the only reason you know about its opposite, peace.

You can only know about any concept because you have its opposite to compare it to. This means that all concepts "exist" only because their opposite is in potential within them. Because the mind can only think in terms of concepts—*is*

16

conceptualization—it means that via the mind you can never know an absolute.

The problem is that as long as you are desire- and ambition-driven and feel the need to become a certain way, you are thinking in terms of absolutes. As no absolutes exist in your experience, this type of thinking keeps you stuck in struggling to achieve the perfect life. Another way of saying this is that you are living a myth. You are living life from the standpoint of a delusion.

To most people, peace and freedom represent *perfection*. Desire and ambition are always beset by struggle; which means that as long as you are aiming for freedom and desiring peace, your experience is the antithesis of these two ideals. This tells you that peace and freedom can never be experienced as long as you think in terms of *becoming*.

Once this is understood, it makes sense to investigate the cause of desire and ambition. Clearly the teachings "you are somebody" are the culprit, for prior to these teachings you simply experienced existing, or being. There were no desires and there was no sense of needing to act in certain ways or to justify yourself to anyone.

You may well say that as a very tiny child you didn't have responsibilities. The question is, why is it that you began struggling as soon as you were given responsibilities? The answer you'll surely come up with is that responsibility equals the need to act, dress, and look in ways that are acceptable to others.

The degree to which you buy into this belief is an indication of how much of your life you live for others. The degree to which you buy into this belief is also an indication of how imperfect you think you are, as you are. In other words, *responsibility signifies the idea of personal control and rejection of what is.*

If, albeit intellectually, you understand that there is no such thing as control, then the idea of responsibility, and its bedfellow guilt, will begin to make less sense to you. However, early on in life you were taught that control is not only real but necessary. Because you adopted the teachings "I am some-body who has the ability to control," and have spent your life considering them to be the truth, this "truth" is a very hard one to let go of.

If you understand that all actions that you undertake happen in relation to what has preceded and combines with them—the actions of others, external events, etc.—you will again realize that personal control is impossible.

This leaves you with the belief "I am some-body." Now, if you-the-person really *exist*, and you are absolutely sure about this, you will feel no need for self-justification. Because self-justification is something you live with day in and day out, it tells you that your existence *as a person* is something you are unsure of— you doubt this form of existence.

Until now you have thought control was something real. If from the preceding process of deduction you are beginning to recognize that you could be wrong, it means that you are ready to take the next step in your investigation.

Because you are constantly in over-reaction mode where your identity is concerned, the belief "I am some-body" is clearly one that is underlain by doubt. This means that the next step of your investigation must necessarily begin with the question: "WHO am I?"

Existence means undoubted presence. If the presence of something is not in doubt another way of saying this is that it is a truth. Now if something is a truth today and not tomorrow, does that mean it has ever been a truth?

If you-the-person exist today and die tomorrow, does that mean your existence was a truth yesterday and is no longer a truth today? Your answer might be that the existence of you-the-person is a relative truth, but *relative* means in relation to something else. Another way of saying this is that the word *relative* does not describe an absolute. This being the case, it means that your "existence" is only temporary.

Of course, you have learned that you were born and will die and this does give you an indication that your existence *is* only temporary. However, you have never had, and never will have an experience of not existing, so you cannot be absolutely certain that this *learned* information about birth and death is the truth.

With some simple, logical deduction, you must look at what *truth* means where you are concerned. When you know something without a doubt, it doesn't matter how much anyone challenges it, you don't over react.

The only undoubted sense you have about yourself is "I exist" or "I am." No amount of challenging of this sense is going to elicit reactionary behavior in you. This tells you that you are in absolutely no doubt about your existence. The only time you over-react is when you-the-person—your appearance and what you do—are challenged.

If you eliminate you-the-person (with a gender, image, age, and roles) from the equation of your existence, you are left with the sense "I exist." As this is the only aspect of your experience about which you hold no doubts, surely it bears looking at a little deeper?

None of the teachings that came subsequent to the knowing "I am" would be possible if this knowing were absent. Isn't it interesting that most everyone, for the majority of their lives, spends their time focusing only on what they have learned about themselves—that they are some-body who needs to become a certain way. How rarely anyone asks, "How do I know that I am?" "How is it possible that I am having this experience?"

If for a moment you turn your focus totally away from what you have learned about yourself towards what you deeply intuit—the sense "I am"—you will experience peace. It doesn't matter what is happening in your life; when you eliminate thoughts about me-the-person and just focus on being, the experience is peaceful.

You will surely have had this experience when you were totally absorbed in an activity.

Retrospectively, you will realize that during such times, when you-the-person, was out of the picture, actions were effortless and uninhibited. Retrospectively, actions will also show themselves to have been more efficient—such as when you totally lose yourself in the task of driving a car and don't know how you got from *A* to *B*.

This tells you that the belief "I exist as somebody" isn't a necessary part of your ability to function. It also tells you, yet again, that what you have learned about yourself is what gets in the way of peaceful, efficient, and effortless actions.

19

Falling in love, getting drunk, going on vacation, immersing yourself in work are some of the many ways people look to transcend focus on the pseudo-self. At such times you feel "I can just be myself," and who and how you think you *should* be is temporarily forgotten.

The question that begs asking is, "Why do you believe the experience of just being yourself is only possible in certain situations?" Your answer may be, "Because I can't be myself when I have to act responsibly." However, if actions happen more efficiently and effortlessly when you-the-person is forgotten, doesn't this tell you that the beliefs you have about responsibility are misconstrued?

IF you are some-body with personal control and your body, mind, and actions are always changing, then most definitely life is meant to be a struggle. If this were true, then you would surely not spend your life aiming for peace. The very fact that you are engaged in this seeming battle, desiring to *become*, means that you doubt that struggle is natural to you. You intuit that peace is the natural experience.

What people rarely realize is that when they have what they want and experience peace, it is never because they have reached their goal. It is because desiring has stopped. As control, desire, and the belief "I exist as some-body" go hand in hand, clearly they are concepts that need investigating.

You experience peace each time desiring, the need to control, and self-consciousness stop. Actions are more efficient and effortless each time desiring, the need to control, and self-consciousness stop. At such times all you are left with is the experience of what is happening. There is no sense of this experience happening in relation to "you." That sense only comes retrospectively when you once again remember yourself. This tells you that when all there is, is experiencing, there is peace.

For control, desire, and self-consciousness to cease, you have to be totally absorbed by what is. You have to be totally present to what is as it is. And what is as it is has to be experienced fully, which will happen quite naturally the minute you lose yourself in any activity.

The problem is that there is absolutely no way you can *deliberately* lose yourself in an activity. Because the only time peace is experienced is when this happens, it means the notion that control can bring you peace is another huge misconception.

This simple line of thinking shows you that it doesn't matter what is happening in your life if the belief, "I exist as some-body" is absent. Even if the activity is deep grieving, immense physical struggle, or intense mental focus on something, when you lose yourself in what is happening you will find that the experience is always underlain by peace.

If you understand this deeply, focus will quite naturally begin to turn away from you-the-person who needs to be in control. Then who you think you are and who you think you should become will gradually or quickly begin to lose meaning for you.

It seems to me that the most worthwhile teaching that has ever been put forward is: "Know Thy Self." This is only possible when you begin questioning everything you have *learned* about yourself and life, and turn your focus towards that which you know without a doubt, "I exist," "I am." This deep knowing, about which you have no doubt, is something you have ignored all your life in exchange for focusing on who you think you should be. This goal-oriented focus has subjected you to a life of struggle, interspersed by brief times when what you have learned about yourself has disappeared because "you" are lost in an activity.

As these brief times are the only times you experience peace, don't you think it is time to re-evaluate what you think of as important—this person you call "me" who is always falling short of your ideals of perfection? Does this person really exist or is he or she nothing more than a misperception adopted in childhood that has left you living your life in the pursuit of acceptance and security?

You experience being and know "I exist." You experience your body, your mind and the rest of manifestation and say, "They exist." Something has to exist before you can know about it.

Did your body, your mind and the rest of manifestation "exist" prior That which knows about them?

Who am I?

You believe you are some-body, and think this is the *truth*.
You believe this person you call "me" exists,
and think this is the *truth*.
What will become of that *truth* when this person is "dead"?

What's been happening since you were here last?

Well, I've always been such a control freak. I've spent most of my life either trying to control, or feeling out of control. Now, since I've been coming here I really seem to have made progress in that area. I'd say I probably only spend fifty percent of the time worrying about control, if that. So I'm feeling a lot more peace.
Are you saying that fifty percent of the time you are quite content with what is going on and have no need to change anything? That's wonderful. So now you only spend fifty percent of the time struggling, and the rest of the time you experience being totally at peace with yourself and the world?!

Well, no. When you put it like that I'd have to say twenty-five percent of the time.
Ah, so your percentage has dropped suddenly! (laughing) But, experiencing peace twenty five percent of the time is good.

Actually, it's probably not that much I guess. When I have decisions to make I don't feel that peace, and I have to make a lot of decisions.
Oops, the percentage has dropped again?! (laughing) You see, it's easy to think that you are going with the flow and less

23

involved in controlling. The thought comes, "I'm not needing to control as much, so clearly I've made progress." When you think in terms of progress what you're actually saying is, "I have more control over my life," isn't it? You think you have let go of the need to control only when you feel in control. But, if that "control" suddenly disappeared, the need would be there all over again, wouldn't it? This means that neediness has never actually been absent. Do you see the paradox?

Yes.
How much of your lives have any of you spent minus the need, or desire, to control? Be clear with yourselves when you think about this. What I am asking is, how much of your life has your mind been free of *shoulds* and *should nots* and desires?

Two percent maybe, if I count when I was a baby. It's probably less than that.
You see, the idea of control has been controlling you all your life! You are a slave to this idea. It is a strong, strong addiction. This means that control is very important to you; so without it what might happen?

The idea of being without any control at all is really scary.
Are you telling me that you have actually *had* control at some time?

Well, temporarily maybe, but I don't think I've ever really had control. It's an illusion.
If you *really* knew control to be an illusion there would be no question of control, no fear about not having it. Probably the fear is that you will never get control; that you will never be in absolute control of life.

Yes.
And yet you tell me you've never really had it anyway. Do you see that you can't be fearful of not having something that you've never had?

But until now I thought control was something I had, even if it was temporary.
Wouldn't you say that the fear comes from not being able to hold onto control? Isn't the fear there because, if you are honest with yourself, deep down you know you can never maintain control?

Yes. But how do I get rid of the fear and the need for control?
Because you are identified with the body and the mind you experience the need to control both. You think these concepts *are* you and that if you control them, "you" will be in control. This is why you experience the need to change how you look, how you feel in your body, and what you think about. The body is changing all the time. Thoughts change all the time. Feelings change all the time. As long as you are identified with something that is constantly changing, the desire for control isn't going to disappear.

So what do we do?
Well, first be clear as to where these thoughts are coming from. Do you cause them? Can you make a thought happen?

No. They just come into my mind.
Do you know where they come from or how they get there? Do you know how the first thought that ever entered your mind got there?

It was programming that I got from my parents. I had lots of programming as a child. My parents were really strict.
And where do you think the thoughts of your parents come from? Where do you think the thoughts of your parents' parents came from? Do you think that anyone ever *made* a thought happen, of their own volition?

No, they can't have.
To realize this is to understand that all thoughts happen *despite* you, not *because* of you.

If you understand that, you'll begin to realize that thoughts happen spontaneously. Thoughts happen despite you, not because of you.

Now tell me about this body you have. How did it come about? Did your parents create it of their own volition? Did they say, "Hey, let's conceive a baby boy next Wednesday"? (laughing)

No.

The coming together of the two parents led to the appearance of this body called Isaac, but your parents didn't have any control over this "birth." They didn't cause it of their own volition. They may have wanted a child, but simply *wanting* never guarantees the desired outcome, however hard you try. Understanding this, it follows that the body you now experience came about spontaneously as a result of the union of your two parents. They were the vehicles that made it possible for this body to appear, but they didn't have any real say in the matter. It was something like a roulette game of chance.

Once you were "born," thoughts spontaneously started appearing—*despite* your parents and *despite* you.

Now let's look at what you call your "birth." You began experiencing being, despite yourself. Your parents' bodies were the instruments for your conception, but that couldn't have happened unless "they" experienced being. Isn't that so?

Yes.

Your parents may have *appeared* to program thoughts in you about control and *shoulds* and *should nots*. This would have been similar to their experience as a child, and that of their parents, and their parents' parents. But as all thoughts happen spontaneously, despite anyone, the thought to teach you happened despite your parents.

Similarly, your mind's receptivity to that programming, or mental conditioning, was something you had no control over—it happened *despite* you. Your parents aren't to blame for it, and you aren't to blame for it.

Both the body and the mind you are now identified with began, not *because* of any-one, but spontaneously. This is the case with all bodyminds. And that's what *synchronicity* means: the coincidence of a chain of events for which there is no discernible reason.

Your "birth" is simply part of a coincidental chain of events, a synchronicity that comes about spontaneously and for no particular reason. Do you see that? Don't just accept what I'm telling you. I'm asking you to think about what I say. You don't have to agree.

No, it makes sense. I can see that control had nothing to do with the appearance of this body or the thoughts that come into the mind. So I'm just an accident? That's what my parents told me too! (laughing)

One could say that your "birth" is just an accident. There is no particular reason for it. If you understand this, the belief in a life's purpose certainly needs some re-evaluation, eh? (laughing)

Once you realize that it's impossible to define a reason for your "birth," the only answer you can come up with when asking how this all came about is that it happened *spontaneously*. Everything about the "you" that is now experienced happened spontaneously. At "birth" you began experiencing being. How did that happen?

I don't know. It just did.

The experience of being is also something that happened despite you, isn't it? You had no say in the matter. You didn't control your "birth." But of course that's what people like to think. That's why they talk about "choosing their parents." This is just comforting New Age jargon. Well, I guess it's comforting if you like the parents you "chose." (laughing)

Wouldn't you say that how you began experiencing life would be the natural state?

Yes.

Did the outset of life contain any thoughts about control?

No.
Thoughts about control came afterwards, isn't that so? When
you began learning about how you should act, think, and be,
then the thoughts about control began to accumulate. As your
mind was empty of such thoughts at "birth," they can't be
called innate or inborn.

*No. But everyone has them. There isn't a person alive who doesn't
develop the belief in control, is there?*
The common progression in a human life is that thoughts of
control come about. I say *common*, rather than natural, because
these thoughts are not innate—you are not born thinking, "This
is how it is!" Just because something is common to everyone
doesn't make it natural. Beliefs about control are common to
everyone, but these beliefs were not inborn, not innate, and not
natural.
Of course, in the context that everything happens despite you,
the belief in control *is* natural. But the idea of personal control
and personal struggle is contrary to your nature; so in that sense
it is unnatural.

But why does that happen? Why does this belief start?
What do you care? If I were to give you a reason would it make
your life any easier? Would it change anything about your life
and your desire to control?

Well, it might make it easier if we knew the reason.
Ah, and how would that be? In what way would it make your
life easier? Would the belief in personal control suddenly fall
away if I gave you a reason for it?
In the very next moment you could have a heart attack and the
sense of being could stop. If that happened, could you say that
the control you thought you had up until that moment was real?

It was relatively real.
The word *relative* means that something has significance in
relation to something else. And the word *reality* means, "under-

lying appearances." As far as I know, the word *appearance* describes a "thing." This means that *relativity* has to do with appearances, whereas *reality* has to do with that which underlies "things." So, how can you put these two words, relative and real, together?

I've looked reality up in the dictionary and it doesn't say anything about "underlying appearances."
In the Oxford English dictionary that is the definition. But you don't need to rely on dictionaries. All you need to do is use some simple logic.
For example, you believe that things *exist*. You think that you are the body and that you-the-body *exist*. When you say, "I exist," you say it with absolute conviction. You know you *are* because you experience being and have nothad and will never have an experience of not being.
At the same time, you have learned about the "death" of the body. So you know that the body will come to an end. As you are identified with the body, this means that "you" will come to an end.
Perhaps you believe that you will actually die. Perhaps you believe you will turn into an angel or a spirit. Either way, the person you now think of as "me"—with its earthly appearance—is going to end or change dramatically at the time of "death."
Right now there is a body sitting here, but imagine that it suddenly combusts and is burned to ashes. Will you still call it a body?

No, it's a pile of ashes.
One moment it "exists" and the next it's gone, or changed beyond recognition. You can say that there *was* a body, but you can no longer say that a body is still there. Eventually all objects change and disintegrate.

That doesn't mean they haven't existed.
Ah, but when you say, "My body exists," is there any doubt in your mind as to the *existence* of the body?

29

No.
When you say, "My body exists," there is no doubt in your mind. And this is the meaning of the word *exist*—it describes irrefutable presence. A presence which is not doubted can also be said to be a truth or a fact, can't it?

Yes.
If I told you something today and said, "This is the absolute truth," and then came back tomorrow and said, "Actually, I was mistaken," what would you think?

I'd think that you had lied to me.
Would you think that the "truth" I told you yesterday *was* a truth, until I told you it wasn't?

No. I'd say that it had never been the truth.
Existence describes undoubted presence. When you have *absolutely* no doubt about something you say, "It is the truth." This means that truth is an absolute. After all it can't be the truth one-day and a lie the next. That would mean it never was the truth.
Existence means undoubted presence, so existence is synonymous with *truth*. As *truth* describes an absolute, *existence* must also describe an absolute.
The body you are identified with will eventually "die." Even if you believe that "you" will carry on as an angel or a spirit, the body—as it now appears—will disappear. As *existence* describes an absolute—an irrefutable presence—how can you say "you" *exist*? That is as ridiculous as saying, "What I told you yesterday *was* the truth, but today it's a lie."
While you are identified with an object, an appearance, you remain in ignorance of Your True nature. Most people intuit that even after "death" they will continue existing in some form or other. Most people find it impossible to conceive of "death" as the absolute end of self. This is why so many believe in the afterlife and such things.
Who you *think* you are is not an absolute and, therefore, does not exist.

Can you repeat that?
Existence describes absolute presence. Who you *think* you are—
the bodymind appearance—has a beginning and comes to an
end. This means that who you *think* you are does not exist.
Most people intuit that there has to be something after "death,"
but they can only think in terms of a conceptual self. This is
why they think they become a spirit or a soul that floats up to
heaven or migrates to another body.
If you don't ignore this intuition, but also don't opt for imagi-
nary solutions, you will become what we call a seeker. To
discover the Truth, you have to find out what is constant about
you—what really *Exists*.

I'm confused.
Yes, all seekers are confused. That is why they're seeking.
(laughing)
Confusion is good because it means your mind has been thrown
off balance. But of course this isn't to say it was actually *bal-
anced* in the first place! (laughing)
What you have given lip service to up until now is being questioned. I don't want you to take what I'm saying for granted. I
don't need you to agree with me. You see many of you have
been coming here because you say you are finding more peace.
In the same sentence many of you have also told me this is
because you are less reactionary. Then you tell me, "I'm only
reactionary when I have to make decisions, or something goes
wrong." This simply means that your intellectual understanding
has helped you have a clearer perspective, for a while.
There is no point in coming here if you just want to cope better.
Coping is all about temporary or pseudo-control. What is it you
want when you come here? What do you want from me? If
coming here is just something that helps pass the time and
makes you feel a bit better there's nothing wrong in that. But,
I'm not here to help you cope or feel a *bit* better.
Ultimately, what is said here may give you temporary relief, but
if you don't yearn for permanent relief you have been missing
the point. You are missing the greatest opportunity—to get out

of this habit of coping and controlling. You are missing the opportunity of seeing the ridiculousness of being identified with this limited "me" idea.

But we like being with you. I don't know how it would be if I couldn't come here once a week. Maybe the effects would wear off.
Exactly. The effects, the coping you are learning, might wear off. As long as you are enjoying coming here to maintain "the effect" you are using being with me in the same way you use an aspirin. What is the use of anything if it only provides temporary relief?

Very little! It's so frustrating though.
Yes, it's frustrating. Right now you have begun to experience more peace, but you admit that it is fleeting—dependent on circumstances. Don't rest on your laurels and be satisfied with that! When you start feeling deep frustration because the changes are temporary and you see they are dependent on coming here, that is when coming here becomes useful.
First the fire of dissatisfaction, the fire of desire to know what underlies these seeming limitations, has to take hold. When this fire catches and becomes all-consuming, it does all the work. It burns away all other desires, all other needs. First the fire has to ignite.

But how can we make that happen?
Ah, the belief in control rears its ugly head yet again! (laughing) You cannot *make* this fire catch light. The lethargy and indifference that began when you started identifying with the body and mind happened *despite* you. Do you think the fire that can consume this lethargy is going to happen *because* of you, or because of anything you do?

It can't, I guess. Yes, I see that.
This fire ignites in but a few cases, but each time I ask you why you are here and what you want from me, what happens?

I get confused. I want to know who I really am. On and off through-

32

out my life I've wanted that, but the desire isn't there all the time.
So, how come it is such an on and off thing?

Well, there are distractions. I have to work and live my life. I'd like to just retire and be, but that isn't possible right now.
Amid all your activities and distractions does the experience "I am" ever cease?

No.
This is a common misconception; that you have to cease living life *as it is* in order to Be. Simple logic tells you that that makes no sense at all.

Yes, but when I have decisions to make or work to do I can't be as present as I want to be all the time.
How can you ever *be* absent? Don't you experience being all the time during the waking and dreaming states? It is a matter of paying attention to whatever you are doing and remembering that none of it could be experienced if you didn't first experience being. When you understand this, there is no need to stop doing anything, is there? It means you are totally *present* to what is.
What needs to happen is that you pay more attention to what is being experienced *because* you experience being. You rarely, if ever, ask how the experience of being is possible. You are so busy trying to control experiences that it never occurs to you to ask, "How is the experiencing of anything possible?" You take this "I amness" for granted because you've always known it, but the ever-changing objects of experience are rarely taken for granted, are they? All the different experiences are rarely taken for granted, are they?

No. But it feels as if experiences affect me.
Right now you have the belief, "Experiences affect me," and you think this is the truth. So let's look at this little word *truth* some more. Would you say that the word truth describes permanency? Or would you say truth is the truth until it is proven to be a lie?

I'd say truth describes permanency. If it's proven wrong it never was the truth; and if it never was the truth, then it's always been a lie.

Of course, everyone has their own ideas about truth. You talk of "half-truths," and when you disagree with someone you might act diplomatically and say, "That's your truth and this is mine." Like all concepts, *truth* is considered a commodity. That's why people talk about "personal truths" as if they can own the truth. On the one hand, people think of truth as an absolute: "This is how it is!" Then, when the "truth" is dis-proven, they shake their heads and think, "Ah well, guess I was wrong."

Now, if they paused to think about this turn-around a little, they would see that simultaneously within what they were calling *truth* there was already *un-truth*. What they considered an absolute turns out to be nothing of the kind.

Paradox.

Yes, paradox. You are identified with the mind and think you *are* it. Because all thoughts are dualistic—this versus that— "you" remain oblivious to paradox. But with a little investigation of the concepts you hold dear, you'd soon find that *all* concepts are paradoxical.

Until the paradoxical nature of life is deeply understood, you continue needing control and thinking it is possible. Because you think in terms of this versus that all the time, of course you are slaves to the idea of control.

Once you begin to realize that control is absolutely beyond your grasp—or control—you realize there is no such thing as control. If this understanding goes deep enough, it disrupts old thinking patterns so much that you start re-evaluating your whole tack on the meaning of life. You begin looking for the real Truth. You *become* a seeker.

The trouble is, while you think in terms of this versus that and "me" versus "others," you can only come up with relative truths. And, of course, relative truths are totally dissatisfying to you. You want to know with *absolute* certainty who or what you are.

34

I understand what you've been doing, but isn't it just playing with words?
Yes, of course. I'm "playing with words," but it's constructive play.
You are slaves to dualistic thinking and the misperception of self is perpetuated by rigid, seemingly contradictory concepts. This has given rise to the need to control, which controls "you."
Once you start questioning the concepts that control "you," you have the possibility of recognizing that they are not a bunch of mutually exclusive, juxtaposed factors. All concepts are inextricably interlinked and *mutually inclusive.*

My mind is aching.
Yes. Until now your rigid thinking mode has kept you under hypnosis, thinking of relativity as reality—appearances as underlying appearances. You may have believed you were thinking logically, but much of the time what you call *logic* is no more than familiar, comfortable thoughts. I'm not saying anything very complicated here, but it is unfamiliar to you. I am following simple logic, but it's not *logic* as you know it. It's totally unfamiliar, so you feel easily overwhelmed.
When this overwhelm happens, it's usually good because you just can't struggle to understand anymore. That's often when the Truth between the words is intuited, and tears start falling. The mind goes blank, but afterwards people come up and say, "I understood something today, but I have no idea what it was." That's when the words have begun filtering beyond the mind.

I know this is a silly question. I'm a bit slow, but this is all new to me. Are you saying that we don't exist as we think we do?
Yes, that's exactly what I'm saying. Your mind holds no truth about Your existence. The "you" that is made up of this pile of concepts is unreal. This pseudo-you is an appearance only, an impermanent appearance—as all appearances are. This means that who you *think* you are—this bundle of labels you call

"me"—doesn't exist. This is because *existence* describes permanency—an unchanging, irrefutable presence.

The only thing irrefutable, beyond doubt, about this "me"-appearance is that it is always changing. The word "me" describes a bundle of appearances, but the mystery to be solved is how is it possible to have the experience of these appearances?

Because I am.

The experience "I am" is the one experience, amid all your experiences, that has never changed as long as you have had a body.

One could say that, from a relative standpoint, this "I amness" is the only irrefutable concept you know of. The trouble is that this concept will also end with the "death" of the body. This "I amness" is the only constant you know of, but if it really *existed*, irrefutably, it would not be subject to termination.

Most everyone intuits that there has to be an absolute Truth with regards to "their" existence. Everyone believes they exist and that there is no doubt about it. Do you doubt that you exist?

No.

If you recognize that the word *exist* describes permanency, you have to look beyond everything you have learned about yourself if you want to find out who, or what, you really are. To find the irrefutable Truth of Your existence you have to look for That which is unaffected by change.

But everything is always subject to change, isn't it?

Yes, every "thing" is subject to change. But you intuit that you won't just come to an end—or at least most people do. So if you are trying to find out who you really are, you have to stop fixating on ever-changing experiences and ever-changing things. You have to look to that which is constant. The only seeming constant you know is *experiencing*. Even though experiencing, or the experience of being, stops in deep sleep and in the waking and dreaming states, *experiencing* is happening all the time. So experiencing is the closest you can come to a constant.

This is why you have to become very, very familiar with this "I amness." It's the only clue or collateral you have where this search for the Truth of Your existence is concerned.

Logic is the science of reasoning and proving, but most people are content to think superficially, taking everything at face value. When they can't prove something they invent concepts that no-one can disprove.

But lots of people have experiences of past lives. And I was watching a program the other day with all these people who had near-death experiences. They all moved towards a light. When they came back most of them were enlightened because they knew they weren't the body.

Oh really! (laughing) Well WHO went towards the light, and WHO came back? That's what I'd like to know. (laughing)

You see you are under hypnosis, deluded by fanciful ideas. You are fascinated by strange phenomena. Sadly, the greatest phenomenon of all—the experience of being—gets very little, if any, serious attention.

But how can we tell what is real, what exists and what doesn't?

Use the mind constructively. *Existence* describes that which is irrefutable, beyond doubt, and unchanging. The mind is void of irrefutable facts.

Reality means underlying appearances, and the mind only has data on appearances. This tells you that the mind has its limitations.

Today we've investigated three concepts that, until now, many of you thought of as absolutes—*control, existence,* and *truth.* If you take time to investigate some of the many concepts you consider to be absolutes, you'll soon discover they are nothing of the kind.

Then what are we left with? We recognize paradox perhaps, but does that change anything?

(laughing) If you fully recognized that everything is paradox you wouldn't be here. You would have realized that life has never been a struggle. What more could you want than a life void of beliefs about control and struggle?

Right now you think only in terms of this versus that. The beliefs you feel certain about you think of as absolutes. "This is how it is!" "I *need* to avoid this so that I can have that." "People should do this, and people shouldn't do that," etc. Now, if you begin to recognize that the mind has no data on anything absolute, you will also begin to realize the paradoxical nature of everything. You'll begin realizing that all experiences are interdependent and synchronized. This is when a huge shift in perception and attitude happens. Dogmatic beliefs begin to fall by the wayside, and the habit of struggling to change what is begins to subside.

You wouldn't believe in the concept of *control* if you didn't also believe in lack-of-control. You wouldn't want control, or even consider the idea of it, if you deeply understood that lack-of-control is the bed partner of control. When you think you have control, you strive to keep it. Why? Because you intuit that lack of control is in potential in that "control." This describes paradox.

I understand that everything is paradox, but that hasn't changed the way I act and experience life.

But if this understanding makes sense to you, if you intuit it to be correct, then surely it deserves more investigation. You intuit that everything is paradox, but if nothing much has changed in the way in which you experience life, it means that this understanding is still superficial.

What you have to do is find out why you continue juxtaposing concepts and needing to control one concept in order to avoid another.

But it's really hard to do that. I don't even know how to begin.

You are in a rut because the mind is full of dualistic thoughts. You cling to your beliefs and consider them absolute truths. One way to get out of this rut is to begin re-evaluating these personal "truths." Just look back over your life and you'll see how many times these "truths" have changed. This simple exercise will give you clear evidence that your "truths" have never been absolutes. This means they have never been the truth.

Truth—in the absolute sense—pertains to reality—to That which is unchanging, permanent. As all concepts relate to change, this tells you that the mind, which is a bundle of concepts, has no information on the Truth.

The mind is the language of paradox. But until now you have thought the mind was the language of absolutes and was capable of knowing the Truth. Worse still, you have probably spent your life thinking in terms of "I know this to be true!" "I know that to be true!"

Although you spend your life interchanging, adopting, and rejecting various "truths," you remain oblivious to the glaring fact that you are incapable of knowing an absolute.

So the mind is the problem then?

Ah, the poor mind. It is always being blamed for everything. No-one stops to consider the fact that without the mind you wouldn't know "I am."

No, the mind isn't a problem. It's just that you are using the mind in an ineffective way. The way in which you are using the mind is the "problem." All that stands in the way of knowing the Truth of your existence is the veil of pseudo-absolutes you are mesmerized by.

To see the pseudo-you for what it is—a faulty perception—you need to recognize that it is not an absolute. There is no truth in it, no irrefutable evidence to support the idea that the conceptual "you" will continue after the "death" of the body.

That the body and mind *exist* is easily refuted, easily disproved, because nothing about them holds true, or is permanent in one particular form, from one day to the next.

So are you suggesting we just go through the dictionary and analyze all the concepts we know of?

My own process was to investigate all the rigid concepts I had been giving lip service to all my life. I loved the study of lan-

guage so this suited me just fine. But it takes a certain nature and intellect to relate to this form of investigation, and not many people are prone to this "path," so to speak.
I don't think it is the only way, but my feeling is that it is the most direct way of cutting through the conceptual mirage. When you come here I explore concepts in this way with you. The benefit of this is not that it will make you continue investigating in the same way, but it may serve to put some chinks in your mental armor.

It feels more like a land mine goes off inside my head when I come here. But at the same time I always feel so much more peaceful. For a while my mind seems to calm down, but then I find myself thinking the same old thoughts about guilt and worry.
The mind has its habitual thoughts and they may not stop overnight. Are you saying that you go away and think in exactly the same way as you always have about yourself?

No. Actually I've begun questioning everything.
And that's all that needs to happen; that habitual ways of thinking begin to show themselves to be faulty, and subject to doubt. The Truth is beyond concepts and so cannot be computed by the mind—which only boots up concepts, can only conceptualize.
When "chinks" start appearing in your mental armor, the Heart is less strongly veiled by the mind. You might oscillate between relief and confusion, but the glimpses of relief give you a strong indication that the Heart is veiled most of the time. Those glimpses happen when rigid beliefs temporarily subside. Temporarily you are able to listen to the voice of the Heart. This is the only voice to listen to. Call it your intuition, whatever you want, but that voice has nothing to do with concepts or logic. It's the gut feeling that grows and tells you that your perceptions and attitudes are missing something.

I feel that so strongly, but it's so painful.
The pain is good. (laughing) If it grows you won't be able to

slip back under complete hypnosis. Then the yearning to "wake up" fully takes hold. That's the fire I've been talking about. We have the concept of *truth* in our language, and tonight you've maybe understood that your idea of *truth as an absolute* is faulty. It's absolutely faulty! (laughing) Yet you intuit that there has to be an absolute Truth where you are concerned, don't you?

Yes.

And for that Truth to be known you first have to recognize the paradoxical nature of all concepts—of everything. You cannot BE the mind, or the body, because they are impermanent, ever-changing. You cannot BE something you say you own—"my body." To BE means to exist, and to exist describes permanency. You know that you ARE, but you don't know how you know this.

This is the mystery you have to unravel. You know you can't be the mind because you cannot be something you experience. To experience anything you have to be separate to it. You know you can't be this taste of "I amness" because you experience it and, therefore, have to be separate to it.

Why do you have to be separate to something you experience? I experience my body. I can see my body. How can I be separate to the body when I experience being in it?

Well, you answer that question. How can you "be in" something and BE it at the same time?

I can't.

You can't "be in" the body *and* BE it. You can't "have" a body *and* BE it.

Who or what is posing the question, "Who am I?" Is it the body? Is it the mind?

It's me—this "I am."

Don't you think the source of the question, "Who am I?" must also be the answer to the question?

41

Can you say that again?
The *source* of the question—as to Your identity—has to BE the answer.

Intellectually I see that, but I still don't know the answer. I still haven't realized the answer.
That you respond to what I say so quickly tells me it is all going straight to the mind. When you start coming here without a head full of agendas and quick responses you may Hear something. That Hearing has nothing to do with the ears or the mind. When your mind is a little freer of conditioned responses, you'll start "getting it" in your Heart.
You haven't "realized the answer" because you still think in terms of some-one asking the question and some-one giving an answer. Who is the one who talks of not having realized the answer? Who knows about having and not having answers? Both knowing and not-knowing are dependent on consciousness—"I amness." If you didn't experience being, you would have no experience of manifestation. Both this "I amness," and manifestation are temporary and will end at the "death" of the body. Understanding this, you must ask who You were prior to these appearances.

How can we ever know that?
You deeply intuit that the "death" of the body can't be the end of you. Misguided "logic" gets in the way of this intuition, but if you are guided by this gut feeling—"I exist and cannot end"— the desire to know the Truth about You will grow. Then your mind will stop getting in the way when you come here. This is the first step, that the mind doesn't take center stage all the time.
Who You really are Is eternal, therefore absolute. You Are the Absolute, Eternal principle in which this whole drama is taking place.
Words come and go, so no word is an absolute. This is why the Truth about Your existence has no verbal explanation. So stop trying so hard to understand—IF you can. (laughing)

The words that come out of my mouth may help put the mind into perspective, but between the words, before and after the words, that's where the Truth Is.

You are not an object having *the experience of a bodymind*. You are *the experiencing of a bodymind and other objects*. Prior to the experiencing of objects were You absent or was there simply the absence of any-thing to experience?

Essential Nature and True Nature

Would you search for something if you were holding it in your hand? .... You are probably answering, "Of course I wouldn't!" Have you-the-seeker ever wondered what is doing the seeking? Have you-the seeker ever wondered why what you seek is called Self?

Am I understanding—are you saying that the mind is Consciousness?
Your True or original nature is beyond concepts—it can't be put into words. But for our purpose, we'll say your True nature is Awareness.
The mind is to Awareness what a wave is to the ocean. And as we are using the ocean as a metaphor for the Absolute, let's think of this ocean as being shore-less. The mind is like a wave on a shore-less ocean.

So the mind is awareness?
Don't go so fast, I'm getting there! (laughing)
First you must be clear that I'm just differentiating between the concepts of Awareness and Consciousness to give you imagery. And do remember that these are just concepts. They aren't a solution or an answer.
Your original nature is Awareness, unaware of it-Self. It is unaware of it-Self because it has nothing to compare it-Self to. The body and all of manifestation arises out of Awareness and contrast results in what is called Self-consciousness.
The mind—a collection of thoughts—reflects You in relation to duality. In the mind, Self-consciousness is reflected in the words "I am." With the onset of interaction with the world, the mind

45

reflects "I am" in relation to the bodymind. These two concepts are then linked together and the notion "I am some-body" begins to take hold. A reflection is the objective appearance of the reflected subject.

To put imagery to this, we'll say Awareness is similar to a totally calm, shore-less ocean. *Objects*—the body, "I amness," and all of manifestation—find form in the *Subject*—Awareness.

Like a wave, which casts a shadow in the ocean, manifestation casts a *shadow* in Awareness. This *shadow* is what we call mind. Do remember I'm just giving you imagery here, nothing real.

When waves cast shadows on the surface of the ocean is there any *real* separation between the ocean, the waves, and the shadows?

No.
Each wave has it's own unique form. Does the apparent difference between waves result in any *real* separation between them?

No, all the waves are water. All the waves are part of the same ocean.
Yes. Now, there are many different types of bodies. Their physical appearance differs and their animation, or the way they function, differs. *In reality* do these differences constitute a separation? Is there any *real* separation between bodies because they look and move differently?

That depends on what you mean by "real."
Reality means "underlying appearances." Because the physical and kinetic appearance differs from body to body, does that mean there is any *real* separation between them?

*Well, if, as you say, Reality underlies appearances, just because physically and kinetically bodies **appear** different it doesn't mean there is any **real** separation between them. Ah, so you could say there **really** aren't any bodies!* (laughing)
Wow, you're **really** catching on fast! (laughing)

46

Relative or *apparent* differences arise in undifferentiated Reality. Manifest-Self, or Self-consciousness, arises in Awareness unaware of it-Self. Now tell me, is there any separation between these two?

Can you repeat that?
Is there any *real* separation between manifest-Self—"I am-consciousness"—and non-manifest-Self?

No. Manifest-Self is, well, it's an extension of the non-manifest-Self.
Yes, exactly! That which preceded and has given rise to "I am-consciousness" is not separate to it. They are not-two.
So, when I say, "Find out who You were prior to the existence of the body," what am I asking you to do?

Well, I'm not the body—although that still isn't my experience. (laughing). So, if I'm not the body, there's just "I am-consciousness." So, to know who or what I was prior to the body.... Well, prior to the body, "I am-consciousness" wasn't there. That means I didn't know I existed. But awareness was there ...
Remember, *Awareness* is just a word I've been using for something which is beyond words. As soon as we put a word to That which is wordless, it is impossible to avoid the connotations of that word. You aren't a connotation and You aren't a concept. *Awareness* is a description only. It's not the solution to You.

Yes, I get that. But ...
Okay. As long as you do "get" that! Go on. (laughing)

Before consciousness of myself, awareness was there but I didn't know it! Consciousness and awareness are not separate. So, by asking me to find out who I was before the body you are asking the impossible! I can only know being. I can't know not being—can I?

47

Ah, that is for you to figure out. I'm just here to derail the mind, set it off track.

Well you are doing a great job! Thank you very much … I think.
(laughing)
While there is a body through which Consciousness expresses it-Self you have to become intimately familiar with this animating principle. You have to discover what this consciousness or "I amness" is, minus all the trappings and identities. This is your first concern. First of all, get to know Your essential nature.

Can you explain essential nature again?
Your essential nature is the expression of Consciousness through the body. Consciousness is the essence of the body.
Formless Awareness is Your True or original nature. Your original nature is infinite and eternal, which means You are everywhere and timeless. If You are everywhere and timeless, will there be any movement in you from one place to another?

No, if I'm everywhere and timeless I'd have nowhere to move to!
Yes. Your original nature is *dimension-less, limit-less,* and *time-less*. Because You are formless, infinite, and eternal, there is nowhere to move to. You aren't bound or limited by any-thing, You simply ARE. You have no dimension or form, so You have no measurable objects to move between.
Out of formlessness unaware of it-Self, the body-form arises and "I am-consciousness" results. You, the Subject, give rise to the objective You, and they are not separate—not-two. There is an *apparent* difference, but no *real* difference between Subject and object.
The word *space* is defined as "continuous unlimited area that may or may not contain objects." But would you know about space if there were nothing to compare it to? Can you talk about space unless it occurs within the framework of objects?

No.
In reality you have no knowledge of space. You only know

about space in relative terms. You only know about space in relation to objects. So, if I say prior to the body you were just empty space, that doesn't tell you anything about the Truth of You. Do you get that?

Yes.
Space is just a concept and You are prior to concepts. Space—the interval between objects—and time—the measurement of that interval—is all you know. Because Your essential nature—this "I amness"—occurs in space-time it appears to have a beginning and an end. But in Reality, is Your essential nature limited by the objects it animates? In Reality, is this "I amness" limited by or to the body?

No, but the body dies and "I amness" ends.
Consciousness animates different bodies in unique ways. Does the unique expression of consciousness happening through one body cause any *real* separation in Consciousness?

No. It's all just Consciousness.
Doesn't that mean that Consciousness is not limited by the body? And doesn't that mean that Consciousness is unlimited—without a beginning or an end?

Yes. But when the body dies, Consciousness ends.
If Consciousness has never been limited by, or to, the body, how can it end?

But it does. You said so yourself. "When the body dies 'I amness' stops."
A particular aspect or expression of Consciousness stops when a body "dies." Someone standing over a "dead" body will see that the *appearance* of consciousness has stopped. But for this perception to happen, there has to be consciousness. There has to be another aspect or expression of Consciousness having this perception.
If there is no real separation in Consciousness between one body and another, has Consciousness *really* stopped?

49

No. But what if all bodies suddenly died and it was the end of the world?
If you have a lump of clay and fashion it into a vase you will say the vase is made of clay. You will not say the vase is made of vase, will you? If you break the vase, the form and it's unique shape are lost, but the substance is still there.
If all bodies disappear, the thought-form, "I am," will also disappear. The unique expression of "I am"—the personality—will also disappear. But will Consciousness *really* end?

I'm not sure what you mean. If consciousness is awareness plus the body, and all bodies disappear, then consciousness ends, doesn't it?
Awareness plus the body equals consciousness. The mind reflects this contrast in the thought "I am." Earlier you agreed that Consciousness is not, and never has been, limited by or to the body. If all bodies suddenly disappeared, "I am-consciousness" would cease, yes. But if the *substance* of Consciousness is Awareness, and they are not-two, how can you say Consciousness can end? Did it ever *really* begin?

Well, it appears to begin when the body is born and appears to end when the body dies.
Yes, Consciousness *appears* to begin and *appears* to end. The key word is *appears*.
Consciousness is an *appearance* that is not separate to Awareness. Awareness or the Absolute assumes an appearance. Spontaneously, the non-apparent assumes an appearance. In this way, one could say appearances give You the non-apparent contrast. Because of this contrast you know about Your Self. This *knowing* is what is called consciousness.
Do you think that You-the-non-apparent are any more than you were before, just because you have assumed an appearance?

No. No, it's only appearances I've assumed so it hasn't really changed Me in any way at all.
Exactly. Although You know about Your Self, You haven't

changed in any way. So, has anything really happened?

Well, I've assumed an appearance. That has happened.
But has anything really happened to You?

No.
And as You are infinite and eternal, You are all there IS. As You are all there IS and you've assumed an appearance that hasn't changed You in any way, has anything really happened.

No.
So although it may seem like I'm playing with words here— which I am (laughing)—what I'm trying to make clear to you is that You have never been "other" than Your original, True nature.
A wave appears in the ocean, but that doesn't change the nature of the ocean—it's still water. The wave has never been anything separate to the ocean—they are not-two. All that has happened is an appearance.
Consciousness *appears* to arise and subside in Awareness. This appearance does not change Awareness or the Absolute in any way because Consciousness is not separate from It. This means that nothing has really happened. Do you see that?

Yes.
If you understand that nothing has ever really happened to You, this may dilute some of the importance you give to all the daily *happenings* you experience.

But life still goes on and we still have to be here! Isn't it good to enjoy life and appreciate it? What is the point otherwise?
Ah, "the point"! (laughing) There is no point, no purpose, and no meaning. While you fixate on "the point" or purpose, everything will take on importance for you. This *seeming* importance keeps you involved. You think of *caring* as something important because you misunderstand caring to mean "something to do with the heart." Even the dictionary

definition of *caring* has nothing to do with the heart. *Caring*, in the dictionary, is defined as "worry, anxiety, heed, caution, and pains." This tells you that *caring* has everything to do with the head, not the heart, doesn't it? (laughing)

But when I say we have to care, I mean heart-caring.
Well, maybe that's what you *think* you mean. But while you are identified with the body and mind, the Heart is not something you really know anything about. You think love has something to do with the heart, but you don't know what love is. You only know about caring in terms of worry.

What do you mean?
Love, for a start, is not an emotion—contrary to common interpretation. In Chinese medicine, for example, the five true emotions are worry, sadness, joy, grief, fear and anger. *Love* doesn't figure in the equation.
You see love is not an *emotion*.

How can you say that? If I love someone I feel strong emotions.
Ah, yes. When you love someone, you feel strong emotions. Initially, those emotions are simply the *joy* of being with that person, and the sweet *sadness* of saying good-bye to them. Underlying those emotions is peace. This peace is the closest you come to knowing Love.
Love is not an emotion. *Love* describes neutrality—the absence of judgments, censorship, desire, and worry.
The trouble is you don't focus on the peace. You focus on the joy and sadness. This is because "you" of all the identities are a drama in your own right—you are addicted to drama. And remember, *drama* is all about play acting—about illusion.
You are identified with emotions—the mind or thoughts—so you focus on them, and they are important to you. You focus on the emotions and call them "love," and you don't want the feelings to end.
As soon as you start focusing on not wanting this pseudo-love to end, you start caring more and more. That is, you start

52

worrying about how to keep the relationship going. Then worry begins, maybe anger, etc. and you repeatedly tell the other person how much you *care*. And caring is what has resulted— worry, anxiety, pain.

You see caring is nothing more than unhealthy involvement. Whereas Love, which is not an emotion, describes neutrality— the absence of judgments, censorship, desire, and worry. Under this definition of *love* can you ever say you have really known Love? I'm sure you *care* a lot, (laughing) but do you know anything about Love?

I guess not. That's so depressing! (laughing)
What *is* "depressing" is the misperception that you *need* to care and that things *need* to matter. You see if you understand that your True nature IS neutrality, caring and making things matter is really missing the mark.

I see. (sigh)
If you understand that nothing has ever *really* happened, life begins to lose its importance. That is, actions will happen with decreasing involvement. This doesn't mean that you will reject life, or become despondent with it. It's quite the contrary.

While you are involved you are despondent much of the time. If you realize that nothing is more or less important than anything else, involvement will dissipate. This means that rather than worrying about what was, what might be, and what isn't, you will begin to see what Is in a clearer light.

While you are identified with the bodymind, you compare and judge it against other bodyminds. The much-touted "virtue" of *caring* results, and that is involvement.

It's hard for me to imagine how you carry on living and experiencing life. I've tried imagining it, but I just can't. Isn't it difficult to continue being here?
While I was identified with the body and mind, that *did* seem difficult! (laughing) Why would life be difficult now that I know I'm not a limited object?

When you were a very tiny child you weren't identified with any object. You experienced uninhibited spontaneity. Even if there were physical traumas, there was no censorship or judgment of them, so you were fully present to *all* experiences. Minus the struggle to change and censor experiences, life was underlain by peace.

But when I was a tiny child I had someone to look after me!
Well I hardly think you were earning a living and buying groceries for yourself! (laughing) You had a tiny body that needed looking after. That is natural. But you still had a taste of yourself as unlimited, uninhibited, effortless, and spontaneous, yes?

Yes.
The difference between your childhood experience and your present experience of self is that now you believe you are the body and mind. So now you experience life as a struggle. Thoughts and actions have always happened despite you. Do you understand that to some degree?

Yes, but I can't really say it's my experience.
The belief, "Actions happen *because* of me," is still fairly strong. As a result you still believe in personal struggle. We could say that struggle is unnatural to you, whereas effortlessness is natural. But in fact, because *all* actions happen despite you, even efforting is *natural.*

But it's not our true nature. I mean it's not our essential nature.
Ah, good, you're getting the differentiation I'm making! No, struggle isn't Your essential nature, you're quite right. I'm just making the point that even though you mistake actions to be personal struggling, those actions are happening despite you. This means that your perception of Your essential nature is faulty. It also means that Your essential nature isn't hidden from you. You just aren't seeing it for what it is. The delusion that actions are personal causes you to experience life as a struggle.

I understand that actions happen despite me, but I still just can't get beyond the programming.
You don't have to "get beyond the programming." You have to see it for what it is—invalid information about You. As this information is invalid, it means it's not the Truth. As the programming "I am some-body" is not the Truth, it means this pseudo-you doesn't exist. So it's not a matter of seeing beyond appearances. It's a matter of having a clear understanding that You are not them.
This is why you must investigate this consciousness and familiarize yourself with it. Find out what it is minus all the labels and trappings.

But how do I do that?
First, you have to be absolutely clear on who You are not. First, you have to be convinced that You are not an object. As soon as you know You are not the bodymind, what is left?

Me. "I am."
Your essential nature is "I am-consciousness" or *experiencing*, minus censorship and inhibition. "I am-consciousness" is the essence or taste of the body. Your True nature is prior to that taste.
You can't know what an onion tastes like without the onion. Similarly, you can't know Your essential nature without the body. Both the body and its "taste"—"I amness"—are the objective expression of the "tasteless" Subject.
Before an onion has onion-form and onion-taste it is a seed. Before You assumed manifest form and its taste, "I am-consciousness," you Are. When this bodily form "dies" and the taste of consciousness ceases You still are.
What you need to discover is what preceded essence and form. What is the *seed* out of which this body and consciousness has sprouted?
If there is no seed, no onion will form. If there is no onion you can't know onion-taste. Without a tasting and perceiving subject, no object can be tasted and its form can't be seen. Are you following me?

55

Yes.
Your original nature is the seed from which the body and mind-forms have sprouted. Your essential nature is the "taste" of this *sprouting*.
Water you drink out of a clay cup will taste different to water you drink out of a tin cup. This doesn't mean that the essential nature of water has changed in any way. It is still water.
Similarly, your personality has a unique "taste" or flavor compared to personalities being expressed through other bodies. But all personalities are, are unique expressions of Consciousness. Personalities vary according to different bodies, but this doesn't change Consciousness in any way. The differences are not real.
Your essential nature *is* Experiencing or Consciousness. Consciousness expresses it-Self in unique ways through each different bodymind. As a result, consciousness or experiencing appears to be different, but the difference isn't a real one. There is no separation in Consciousness. That you believe you are an island unto yourself is a misperception.

It's so hard to understand this and not really know it.
Yes. This is why you need to get to know this consciousness and it's *pure* taste.
Right now the *taste* of "you" is objectionable and you want to spit it out. You want to get rid of the feeling of being limited. You want to get rid of guilt and fear.
But there is nothing to get rid of. You simply have to understand that the objectionable taste—this false "you"—isn't real. It doesn't exist.
We could say the taste of Your essential nature is uninhibited spontaneity. You think you are a bodymind and compare yourself to other bodyminds. This comparing of "you" against "others" gives rise to the importance you give to intellect, body image, and the way you talk and act. The importance you give this false "you" gives rise to guilt, pride, fear, and the experience of limitation and struggle. The taste of this false

"you" hasn't changed Your essential nature in any way. Actions are still happening spontaneously and uninhibitedly—despite you—even though you believe otherwise.

It's like someone who has never tasted an apple. He thinks, "It won't have any taste unless I first cook it and add spices to it." He cooks the apple, mixes cinnamon, sugar, raisins and other fruits in with it. Then he tastes this concoction. Will he be able to experience pure undiluted apple-taste?

No.

No, he won't! Apple-taste isn't absent, but because he has added so many other ingredients he doesn't, he can't, have a direct experience of what apple tastes like.

Can this poor deluded cook now extract apple-taste from his mixture?

No.

If he tried to get rid of all the additional ingredients he'd have to throw the apple away too. If he tried to get rid of all the additional tastes he'd lose the apple-taste along with them.

One could say that the *taste* of Your essential nature is spontaneous, uninhibited Self-expression. This expression occurs via bodies that have different appearances and ways of acting. You have identified with these differences. You think, "I am this and that," and the undiluted taste of "I amness" is diluted, or masked, by these identities.

If you are here, it's because you are beginning to feel dissatisfied and frustrated with the distorted taste of "I amness." You can't get rid of these distorted tastes. If you did that you'd also lose the pure, undiluted taste of You. So what needs to happen?

I'm not sure. I'm a bit lost.

Let's say that our cook has tasted apples before. He will know, beyond a shadow of a doubt, that apple-taste isn't cinnamon- and raisin-taste, yes?

57

Yes.
Well, as a newborn infant the taste of Your essential nature was undiluted. Then that taste was reflected in the mind in "I am." Gradually, to this taste of "I amness" you added other ingredients and began to think "I am this and that." But in the early stages, before you added "this and that" to the equation "I am," the taste of Your essential nature was undiluted.
So, like a cook who has experienced the taste of apples, you *have* experienced the undiluted taste of Your essential nature. Now and then when you forget yourself, retrospectively you know that actions happen spontaneously and effortlessly—despite you. When this happens, fleetingly, you get to savor the undiluted taste of Your essential nature and you experience it as peaceful.

Very fleetingly, and rarely! (laughing)
Ah, but don't disregard those glimpses. Pay attention to them because those momentary, undiluted tastes of Your essential nature give you the clue you are looking for. You experience spontaneity, and it is peaceful because the mind isn't booting up thoughts about "I should do this" or "I shouldn't be doing that."
When inhibitions return they do so spontaneously—despite you. This means that Your essential nature isn't absent or hidden from you. It's just that these thought-ingredients mask or dilute the "taste" of spontaneity.
Get enough undiluted "tastes" of Your essential nature, compare them to the usual taste you have of yourself, and you will crave more. This is when the yearning to know the Truth about Self takes hold.

So is it like a craving, or an addiction then?
Yes, you become obsessed with wanting to know the *pure* taste of You. The trouble is that most people try to reject the body and mind as if they were obstacles. That would be like pushing the apple aside because you think it's an obstacle to knowing apple-taste.
It's not the body and mind that are the problem. They are the

mediums for this taste of "I am." The false identities, the other ingredients and tastes you have added to "I am," are all that is getting in the way of knowing the undiluted taste of this "I amness."

But the body, mind, and personality haven't disappeared to you, have they?
No. And they don't have to disappear before I can taste My essential nature.
The taste is always there, undiluted. But while you mistake the added ingredients—the body, the mind, the personality—to BE You, you don't know this.
You seek the Self, believing that the recipe of You is missing something. All you need to understand is that your recipe has just become way too complicated. Self is not missing from the recipe, but until you put the other ingredients into perspective you don't know this.
Goodness, I feel like Martha Stewart! (laughing)

Except that she always has everything in its place and you cause total chaos. (laughing)
Did you know that the root of the word *chaos* is "original unformed universe"?

No.
Well there you go. That will give you something more to ponder, eh? (laughing)

As if we didn't already have enough! (laughing)

I Am the riddle
You seek to solve.

I Am the Questioning,
And it's Source.

I Know who I Am, but tell me,
What about you, ...
Are you any-body?

EV

God and Religion

A lot of people around here are triggered by you because they see you as being anti-religion. I brought a couple of people here, but they said they wouldn't come back because you made them so angry.

No-one can *make* anyone angry. If someone feels anger it's because a belief, an involvement they have, has been triggered by something someone else does or says. Noone over-reacts because someone else *makes* them do so. People only over-react because they feel insecure in the face of something that challenges their beliefs.

But, because you are anti religion makes them feel angry, so really you do cause them to feel that way.

Ah, is that so? (laughing) What makes you think I'm anti-religion?

You talk about their being no God. I have heard you talking about your having had to give up the concept of God.

I'm pretty sure you have never heard me say, "There is no God." As far as "giving up" the concept of God, that isn't something I did voluntarily. The concept of God just fell away. Hopefully by now you have got from what I say that there is no such thing as free-will or personal will power.

Yes, I do understand that, but you did say you had to give up the concept of God.

I still have a functioning mind—however feeble it may seem at times (laughing)—and so concepts are still alive and kicking. It's just that no concept holds any truth for me anymore. The concept that remained the strongest was the one of God. I never thought of God as a man with a long white beard up in the clouds. I

61

simply had a deep sense of God or the Divine since I was a tiny child.

During my twenties I battled with that concept because I couldn't reconcile what I felt in relation to what I had been taught in church. But in my thirties, despite me, the deep sense of something more powerful than "me" resurfaced in full strength. I still couldn't make head nor tail of it, but my heart feeling was stronger than my mental conflict.

Did you start going to church again?
I've always loved churches and cathedrals, but when they were empty. I found them wonderful places to just sit. But no, I never went to church services again.

But if the concept of God has fallen away then you are anti religion?
To be *anti* something you have to have very strong beliefs and feelings about it. To be anti something you have to be very involved. You have to have a vested interest and a strong agenda before you declare yourself anti anything, don't you?

Yes, I guess so.
If right now you knew, without a doubt, that you are not an object or any concept, do you think you would feel anti anything?

I don't know.
Think about it. If you are not an object, and you know this without a doubt, why do you think any object or concept would hold importance for you?

Well, doesn't your family still hold importance for you? Would you be sitting here talking to us if you didn't think it was important?
This body has a stronger link to those of family members. I know those bodies aren't important, but the relationship between this body and their bodies continues. I fully appreciate this relationship, but it doesn't have the importance I once gave it.

As far as, "Would I be sitting here talking to you if I didn't think it important?" that is another matter. I'm here because this is the event that is unfolding. If I was here because I thought it important that you hear what I have to say, that would mean I have a strong agenda and involvement.

I'm not here for any *reason* at all, it's just what's happening. On the surface, the *reason* may seem to be because some of you asked me to do this. On the surface, the *reason* you asked me may seem to be because of this or that. In the end, stuff just happens and it's all part of the whole synchronicity of manifestation, which happens despite anyone.

It's because you give pseudo reasons to everything, and importance to those reasons, that there's such confusion. When you stop giving reasons and looking for meaning you'll just live life and the whole struggle will be over.

You don't look for reasons when you are feeling peaceful; well, not until you start feeling guilty about it. (laughing) That tells you that peace and the search for meaning and *reasons* can never be experienced simultaneously.

I experience peace when I'm in church.
What church do you go to?

Catholic.
Do you experience peace when you are taught you were born in sin and have to do penance for those sins?

No, but I have faith and that gives me peace. People have to believe in something! They have to have faith!
You were not "born" believing in anything. You weren't "born" believing in God.

No, but when I heard about God I knew it was true and my faith in that brings me peace.
My sense is that there are two different kinds of faith. One form of faith is all about hoping. You learn you are born in sin but you also learn that God or Jesus will save you, and that gives you hope. This hope is often called *faith*.

Without hope, without faith, what is there?
You tell me. Before you learned about God and that you needed saving, what was there?

I just was. Then I started growing up, became an adult, and life's difficult and my faith sustains me through the hard times.
And if you had never learned about God—as many people have not—and didn't have your faith, would the hard times be insurmountable?

I don't know. I'm sure with friends and family I could get through them, but I'm sure at least that hope would be there. Hope to overcome the hard times.
When something is happening that you don't like you hope that it will change. This means that hope signifies a rejection of what is. As life is never static, and there are always ups and downs, the downs are as much a part of life as the ups. If every time you experience "downs" you spend your time hoping they will end, that means you are rejecting an aspect of life, doesn't it?

But no-one likes the down times.
Probably not, but they are still a part of life. If you believe that God gave you this life, as it is, doesn't rejection of the down times signify a rejection of God's gift to you?

But God wants us to overcome. He doesn't want us to be unhappy. It's our own fault that we are unhappy and that's why we have to overcome the down times. He gave them to us so we could learn from them.
If that is the case and God gave you the down times so you would learn from them, how are you going to learn anything about down times if you spend every moment of them praying and hoping for them to be over?

That's why faith is important, because we have to have faith that God will help us overcome.

64

If your feelings about the bad times are your "fault," as you say, that means you *make* yourself feel bad. IF you have the personal power to make yourself feel bad, it would seem to me you should be able to make yourself feel good again. But you are saying God does this. Do I understand you correctly?

Yes.
Are the bad times the problem, or is it your feelings about the bad times that are the problem?

Both.
If you didn't struggle against the bad times, would you feel bad?

*I struggle **because** I feel bad.*
And does the struggling make you feel better?

No.
Doesn't that tell you that the bad feelings and the struggling are one and the same? And if struggle and feelings you don't want are one and the same, surely minus them the "bad times" wouldn't be a problem, would they?
You see, that is where we began. No situation and no-one can *make* you feel good or bad. It is only when you have strong beliefs about a situation, such as, "It shouldn't be like this," that you experience reactionary feelings.
One type of *faith* is the kind that is based on hope and the belief that life *should* be better than it is. The other kind of *faith* is simply a deep sense of awe towards what is, as it is. This feeling of awe fills the heart and it doesn't matter what is going on in your life, you trust that it is fine just the way it is.

Isn't trust and hope the same thing?
If you trust in the sense of "the power of positive thinking," it means you are using the mind to block out fears. That is a desperate kind of trust. I'm not saying that the power of positive thinking isn't very useful, but only as an intermediate tool when self-esteem is very low. Once self-esteem is strong enough you

soon realize that it takes more than superficial changes in your belief systems to bring about deep and lasting change in the way you experience life.

If you trust because you deeply sense that what is as it is, is just fine, that's very different. That kind of trust comes from the heart and it doesn't matter what thoughts pop into your head. If that sense is deep enough, it's the heart, not the mind, that you follow.

But I believe in my heart that God is real and that my faith in Him is real.
Is it that you *believe* this in your heart or that you *feel* this deeply in your heart?

I feel it deeply.
Then be guided by those feelings. Are those feelings someone has taught you to have? Has someone *made* you have those feelings?

No.
And from what I understand, those feelings bring you a sense of peace. What you have learned "that you are born in sin and need to be saved," is a belief that can't possibly bring you peace. What this belief has done is superimpose the hoping type of faith on top of your deep knowing.

If you have come here believing I am anti-religion, and yet still persist in coming, that tells me this knowing is there. If only religious dogma guided you, you would have left feeling angry and wouldn't have returned, like your friends.

I don't really understand why I come. I'm trying to understand what you say and keep an open mind, but I do find it very confusing.
On the one hand, my words may seem in conflict with what you believe. On the other hand, if learned religious dogma hasn't totally masked inner knowing, you will also experience the energy behind my words. This energy resonates with your inner knowing. The confusion is an inside job, which was already un-

derway the minute learned dogma was superimposed upon intuition and knowing.

What happens here is that this inner dichotomy is being highlighted. It's not that I *make* you feel confused. I just provide a mirror of what is going on inside you.

But what you say conflicts with most religious beliefs.
What I say conflicts with peoples' *interpretation* of religion. What I say doesn't conflict with the roots of any of the ancient religious teachings. What I say conflicts with the distorted interpretations that have been put together over the years by people who needed to feel powerful and special.

Isn't it Jesus who said, "Of mine own will I canst do nothing"? It's been a long time since I read the Bible, but those words are in there. What I do know is that "Thy will be done" is in there time and again. I don't think any of the prophets said, "Of mine own will I cans't create my own reality." (laughing) What "Thy will be done" infers is that everything happens despite you, which is what I say all the time. So I'm not contradicting religious teachings there.

When I say guilt is not natural to you, or necessary, I'm also not contradicting root teachings. "Thy will be done," means everything happens *despite* you. That being the case where is there room for guilt? So I'm not contradicting root religious teachings there either.

Contemporary teachings about guilt and personal will are interpretations that have come about to give egocentric preachers a sense of purpose and a reason for doing what they do. And don't get me wrong, I have met and listened to many religious teachers who, despite what they might teach, do so from the heart. In such cases, it's the energy behind their words that touches others. The words are unimportant. They teach from their deep sense of "something greater than themselves."

But that deep sense tells us there is a God.
That deep sense tells you that there is something greater than who or what you *think* you are. If this deep knowing is there and religious bigotry and distortions don't mask it totally, it has the

power of gradually whittling away your beliefs in this pseudo you.

But why would religions have come about if they weren't necessary?
Initially religious teachings arose in relation to the deep sense of something greater than the "me." These were then distorted by those who couldn't reconcile with the idea of life happening despite them—beyond their personal control. The religious wars and judgmental behavior that have come about between religious factions and peoples are simply a reflection of the inner battle between what is intuitively known and the beliefs people have.
The mis-interpretations that have been given to the various world religions have come about because man wanted to have a reason for everything. If you ask me, the religions that teach you that God created you sinful, so that He can save you depict a pretty sadistic God.
Why anyone would worship a God who decided to create misery so He would have something to do is beyond me. But it makes sense that egocentric preachers who need to have a meaning and reason for living might read the words "....and God created man in His image," and conclude that God, too, had a reason behind what He did.
It's the belief that everything has to have a reason that is one of the main problems.

But there has to be a reason, or why else would we be here?
Just imagine if you didn't have to be here for any particular reason and you deeply knew it. Don't you think that would take a lot of pressure off you? Ah but then again you might get bored, eh? Perhaps that's why people think God needed to create sinful people, so that He'd have a challenge that would stop Him from getting bored up there. (laughing)
When you spontaneously do something "just for the heck of it," without having any premeditated reason, how does that feel? Does that ever happen to you?

Yes it does. Sometimes afterwards I regret it and it feels really awful. Sometimes it feels really good.

Ah, but *at the time of the action* are you worrying about what you're doing? If you are acting without premeditation, then you won't have any expectation about outcome, will you? Doesn't whatever you are doing, when it happens spontaneously, happen minus concerns *at that time?*

Well yes, but afterwards I can regret doing it.

Afterwards, maybe, when you start asking yourself, "Why the heck did I do that?" or telling yourself "I should have done that differently." Afterwards, when you start looking for meaning and reasons, afterwards you feel regret. But while the spontaneous, uninhibited, un-premeditated action is happening there is peace, isn't there?

Yes.

Sometimes what you are doing is retrospectively seen to have been detrimental, or seems wrong. Then you feel confused and upset. While you are acting with full focus and putting all your energy into it, minus judgments, there is peace.

You see, peace is there when you experience what is as it is fully. Peace is absent the minute you start trying to understand what is and interpret "how it seems to be."

But if I were to lose my temper and kill someone, that would be what is. There's no way anyone is going to see that act as other than bad.

In certain areas of the world a very different value is placed on human life. Very different "laws" exist in different areas of the world. What one culture sees as bad, another finds quite acceptable. You may say they are wrong, but who made you the morals police? Who's to say your beliefs are better or more correct than anyone else's.

But if someone commits incest let's say, noone can find that acceptable?

In some cultures the father initiates the daughter sexually. Because that is part of the culture, the child isn't traumatized by it and the father doesn't feel any guilt.

In our culture, such behavior is seen to be unhealthy. When it happens, very often the perpetrator, having been brought up learning about "incest" as bad, enacts it violently or with feelings of guilt. This violence and the energy behind the action traumatizes the child.

Are you condoning incest then? Do you think it's okay?!
I'm not condoning and I'm not rejecting. I'm simply pointing out that what is considered right action in one culture is often considered totally unacceptable in another. The actions themselves aren't the problem. It's the belief systems that accompany actions that are the problem.

Stuff happens, and it happens despite anyone. It may *seem* as if murder is premeditated, but the thoughts that led up to that murder happened despite the perpetrator of the murder. It may seem that one particular motive or reason triggered a murder but—like any other action—if murder happens it is just part and parcel of the whole synchronicity of events happening in Totality.

On the surface, anything can seem to have a reason, but that is when you look at life through the filters of your beliefs. On the surface, everything can seem to have a reason behind it, but that is when you are looking at life from the "me" versus "others" perspective.

If someone were to hurt your child, wouldn't you get upset? You'd see your child and the person who hurt him, wouldn't you?
If I had a child and someone hurt that child, of course, I'd see the two bodies involved. I'd probably feel tremendous distress if my child was hurt.

But that means you see others and you also react!
Of course I see others. I have a body and you have a body, and I see them both. If you get up and hit the person next to you, I may react. Reactions are quite natural. If I burn myself, I react. If I

hear beautiful music, I might react.

I still see others in the sense of seeing other bodies and I still react. The difference is that I know without a doubt that essentially there are no "others" and there are no differences. The differences are relative only, but they have no Reality to them. Because this is my experience, I don't over-react to anything that happens around me.

Isn't there a fine line between reactions and over-reactions?
Outwardly, when I react to something it may look like an over-reaction, that's for sure. If something happens, there is a strong reaction, because I don't see any need to censor my feelings, they are expressed fully. Outwardly, my behavior might give you the sense that I am over-reacting if you see anger happening that continues for a while. Inwardly, what is happening is that anger comes up. It isn't censored and is experienced and expressed fully because of this. As a result, it subsides as quickly as it came. But if more thoughts about the situation resurface, more emotions may resurface. Because neither the thoughts nor the emotions are censored, again the anger is experienced and expressed fully.

The thoughts and emotions aren't a problem, but if you try to reject or maintain them, that is what leads to over-reaction. The thoughts and emotions become a vicious cycle, perpetuated by the need to control them.

What's the difference when we experience anger then?
If you believe in guilt and you believe that anger is bad, when anger happens your beliefs about it and the situation will cause you to try and censor the emotion. This means you aren't experiencing or demonstrating the anger fully because you are trying to control or make sense of it. As long as you are trying to stop emotions and thoughts because of your beliefs about them, you stay stuck in over-reacting. The emotion and the thoughts don't come and go, but are fueled by underlying beliefs about censorship. As long as you are trying to reject what is happening, you are in over-reaction mode.

Let's say you are grieving the death of a loved one. Chances are your memories, your fears, your regrets keep the grieving going. Then suddenly someone says something that makes you laugh. Temporarily you have been distracted and the grief subsides. Why does it subside?

Because I've been distracted.
You were distracted from all the worrisome thoughts that kept the grief going. The loved one is still "dead," but because, temporarily, you stopped thinking about what was missing, the grief stopped. When the thoughts resurface you'll probably start grieving again. This tells you that events don't cause over-reactions. It's the thoughts you have about those events that cause you to over-react.

If someone I love "dies" there may well be grieving. Thoughts may come, as they do for you, but because I don't cling on to those thoughts or try to stop them or the emotion, the grieving isn't an over-reaction. There is a reaction, or a series of reactions, but there is no involvement.

But if you're grieving there's involvement, surely?
Involvement is only there if you are trying to hold onto or reject what is. If you experience what is as it is, there's no involvement. If there's a reaction to an event, the thoughts and emotions will be as much a part of what is as the event. It's all experienced fully with no sense of needing to change, cling, or reject any aspect of it. That is non-involvement, but there can still be reactions. It's simply that there is no over-reaction.

Ah, okay, I see what you mean.
If you feel confusion and try to reject it, involvement will happen and over-reaction will lead to more confusion. If the confusion is just experienced and you don't give it any importance, it will come and go and maybe even come back again. It's when you give experiences importance that behavior becomes reactionary— an over-reaction. Confusion isn't a problem, but if you give it importance, then it becomes one.

But it feels terrible.
I don't always only have wonderful feelings either. But because I don't give those feelings more or less importance than any other feeling, they don't last.

My faith and my religious beliefs have been important to me all my life. I can't imagine that changing. I still feel the need for them. They feel very important.
IF anything really *is* important do your thoughts about it make it any more or less so? What is the value to giving something importance?

If you think something is important, you respect it and cherish it.
IF something really *is* important, another way of saying this would be that it is valid, don't you think? It's a truth, an important truth.

Yes.
If what you believe about something is true, valid, and important, does it matter what other people think about it? If other people think otherwise does this make your truth, and its importance, any the less?

No.
So if someone knows, without a doubt, that their religious beliefs are true, valid, and important, why will they care what others think? Why will they feel anger if someone says something that conflicts with those beliefs?

Because they see the other person as putting their beliefs down.
Didn't you agree that something really true, valid, and important cannot be changed by people's beliefs?

Yes.
If this is the case, why would anyone be concerned about what anyone else thinks?
You know that you are breathing right now. If I say, "You're not breathing. I don't believe you are," are you going to think I'm putting your belief in breathing down?

73

No, of course not. I know I'm breathing. That's very different to saying, "Guilt is unnecessary."
What is the difference between me challenging your belief, "I am breathing," and me challenging your belief "guilt is necessary?"

I'm confused.
I tell you, "You aren't breathing, Amy." This doesn't cause you to over-react and you don't feel any need to change the way I think, and you aren't triggered by what I say. Maybe you think I'm stupid, but there won't be a charge.
I tell you, "Everything happens despite you, and guilt is unnecessary and not possible." This challenges you and you feel the need to argue the point.
Why does one comment, which challenges what you know, leave you un-charged? Why does another comment, which challenges what you believe, cause a reaction?

What I know and what I believe are two different things. I have always experienced breathing, but I learned to believe about guilt.
Yes. If something is your experience and you haven't needed anyone to teach you about it, it is a knowing. If you believe something, it is because someone has taught you about it.
There are many, many different beliefs flying about with regard to God, religion, will-power, guilt, and blame. You have learned one set of beliefs that say, "This is how it is!"
You come here and hear words that seem to contradict your set of beliefs. Until now those beliefs seemed important and valid for you. Does that mean you know those beliefs to be true? Does that mean there is no shadow of a doubt in you about those beliefs?

No, there isn't.
You have no shadow of a doubt that you are breathing, and so my comments about whether or not you are don't challenge you. You say there is no shadow of a doubt in you about your religious beliefs and yet my comments challenge you. What is the difference Amy? If you have absolutely no doubts, why do you care what I say?

I don't know. Perhaps because some of what you say sounds good. I mean, it would be nice not to have guilt.
If, without a shadow of a doubt, you believe that guilt is necessary and that guilt is what God *decided* for you then surely you must embrace guilt.

I don't have to embrace it. It's just a fact of life.
If something is a "fact of life" and you would prefer it to be otherwise, doesn't that mean you are rejecting an aspect of life? If God gave you life and decided you need guilt, and you would rather not have it, doesn't that mean you are rejecting God's will?

I accept God's will, but I can't embrace guilt. I don't need to.
Let's say you go to the doctor and he says you have a malignant tumor. He tells you, "It's a fact of life for you now, and there's nothing you or I can do about it. All you can do is have faith that it might go away."
If you have a tumor but would rather not have it, does that mean you are *accepting* the tumor? Surely it means that you are, perhaps, resigning yourself to the tumor?
If you know without a doubt that guilt is God's will and that your faith that it will go away is important, isn't another word for that kind of faith *resignation*?

No. Anyway, guilt and a tumor are very different, so I don't get your analogy.
Your doctor may have misdiagnosed you and perhaps the tumor is benign. Because you don't want to believe this bad news, maybe you look for a second opinion. Perhaps the second doctor tells you that you have nothing to worry about. "You were misdiagnosed."
All you have to go on are two contradicting opinions. Maybe you go to other doctors and get more contradictory information. What are you going to do? Who are you going to believe?

I don't know. Perhaps I'd have the tumor removed anyway.
Ah, but the doctor has told you there is nothing he can do.

Then I don't know.
I would listen to my body. I'm sure I would eventually be able to tell what was going on just by paying attention to my body.
Yes, that would probably be your only option, eh? Just monitoring your own experience.

Now what happens because someone has told you that guilt is "a fact of life." You have been taught to "just have faith and you'll be saved," but who is to say this information is correct?

You clearly don't like the idea of guilt, and yet, unlike the tumor, you resign yourself to the idea that it's necessary. I come along and give you another way of looking at life, one that "sounds good." Now you have two conflicting sets of teachings. How can you be sure which of them is correct? How can you be sure either of them is correct?

But the Bible is the word of God.
In the Bible it says, "Thy will be done." In the Bible it says, "God is omnipotent and omnipresent." In other words, Biblical teachings tell you that God is all-powerful and everywhere. From somewhere in the Bible you have understood it to be said that you have personal will-power and are guilty. If these two doctrines are both valid and God's word, then isn't "God's word" full of contradictions?

Why? God gave us the power to make choices so that we would learn.
If something or someone is all-powerful, how can anyone else have any power at all?

But free-will is the test God has given us. He has given us some power so that we can learn to use it properly.
Change the word *power* to *control*. What you believe is that God has ABSOLUTE control, but has given you *a little* control too. Does that make sense to you?

Yes.

If you had absolute control, would you create misery, guilt, fear, and mayhem? Maybe that would stop you from getting bored? (laughing)

You have been taught about a judgmental God who has set you tests. If you fail, He'll punish you, and if you pass the tests, He'll reward you. It seems to me this relationship between you and God can only be likened to sadomasochism.

You believe that these doctrines are valid, true, and important. IF this is the case and we are all nothing more than hopeful masochists awaiting the will of a judgmental God, what does it matter what any of us believe?

I think you are distorting it. God is forgiving.
Judgment and forgiveness are synonymous. You can't forgive someone unless you are simultaneously in judgment of them.

But if you forgive someone it means you stop judging them.
When you say, "I forgive you," all you're really saying is, "You did something wrong and I'm willing to forget it." You aren't saying "you did nothing wrong," are you? To say that you forgive someone is essentially saying, "The wrong-doing is a fact, but I'm willing to over look it!" That sounds like a pretty backhanded proposal to me! How condescending! (laughing)

But I'm not debating your beliefs versus mine. What I'm asking you is: IF your beliefs are true, important, and valid for everyone and guilt is necessary for everyone, does it matter what *anyone* believes? Will conflicting beliefs change the "fact" that guilt is necessary IF it is? If someone believes, "There is no God" and they are wrong, will their belief cause God to disappear?

No.
Now if I tell you "Amy you aren't breathing" will this cause you to stop breathing? Will you become scared and confused and worry about what I say?

No.
You see, you only feel confusion, anger, and fear when there is doubt, or if something you value appears to be in jeopardy.

When I talk about there being no free-will and say guilt is unnecessary, you feel confusion. Others feel anger and don't return. Some tell me they experience fear. This tells you that what I say stirs up doubts and the sense that what you believe in is in jeopardy.

If you know, without a doubt, that your religious beliefs are absolutely valid—in the same way you are certain you are breathing—you won't over-react to anything I say that contradicts those beliefs. You only over-react to comments that stir up your own doubts. If doubt isn't there, there will be absolutely no over-reaction. Do you understand what I'm saying?

Yes.

Even if I said, "You have to believe me!" you wouldn't react or feel confused IF you were absolutely confident in your own beliefs.

I have no vested interest in you taking my words as truth. I know that nothing I say is an absolute truth.

You are saying guilt isn't necessary and that we don't have free-will at all. That sounds as if you are saying your beliefs are more correct than mine! And if you don't have a vested interest, why do you talk about it at all?

The relative difference between you and me is that you experience life as a struggle whereas I don't. You experience guilt, and I don't.

You believe guilt is necessary because it makes you a more responsible person. In other words, you think of guilt as a virtue.

I don't experience guilt, but the absence of guilt hasn't caused me to go around raping, pillaging, and disregarding the feelings of others.

There are people here who asked me to give talks because they recognize that guilt and struggle aren't benefiting them. Like you, they have their doubts and fears, but they are open to looking at alternatives, so I talk. I don't talk from the standpoint of a belief system. I talk from the standpoint of my experience. Some may benefit from being here and some may not. I don't need anyone to believe me. If they choose to listen and it triggers them to investigate their own experience deeper, that's fine. If they don't, then that's fine too.

You see Amy, my background contained similar religious teachings to yours. For a while those teachings felt in such contradiction to my sense of God that I simply decided on agnosticism. I couldn't find any answers within myself and I couldn't find any answers in religion.

What kept me coming back to what I called God was this feeling I had in my heart since a tiny child. Nothing about that feeling gave me any indication that it had anything to do with judgment or guilt. I sensed that there was something greater than me—who I thought I was—but no words, not God, Allah, Jehovah, or any of the teachings that went along with them sufficed to explain what I felt.

One day I simply gave up trying to understand. When that happened, the person I thought I was showed herself to be nothing more than a misperception. The abyss I had felt between "me" and God was gone.

You stopped believing in God altogether then?
"God" was the description I had given to the sense of something greater than me. When I realized I wasn't this "me" called Esther all other concepts were invalidated along with her. This includes the concept of "God."

The sense "I exist" is the same sense happening through all bodies. It seems to be different only because you add descriptions to "I exist" and say, "I exist as some-body." "I exist in such and such a way."

Consciousness or experiencing is necessary for anything to be perceived. Without the sense "I exist" nothing can be experienced. This means that manifestation "exists" within, and because of, Consciousness—not the other way round.

Although no concept makes any sense to me anymore, if I were to give another name to Consciousness, I might call it God. Whatever word I put to It, it makes no difference.

Are you saying you ARE God then?!
What I'm saying is that I am not a concept. *God* is a word, a concept, which has been attributed to that aspect of human experience that cannot be explained. The sense of something greater than the small self is what has been called God. When you fully realize that you are not this small self, the experience of something greater than you disappears.

The misperception that "I am some-body" has gone. While that sense was there it was accompanied by the sense of something greater than "me." Now that "me" is seen for what it is—nothing real—what do you think remains?

I don't follow.
Before it seemed that there was "me" and God, and I thought the separateness I felt was real. Now the illusory "me" is seen for what it is—an illusion, a faulty perception. The sense of separateness has disappeared. All there is, is Consciousness, and you can call that God if you want to.

The unique expression of Consciousness happening through your body is the same Consciousness as that expressing through my body. While Consciousness expresses it-Self in manifestation, it has attributes that can be described.

What do you mean?
Consciousness expresses it-Self in various ways through various bodies. These ways or attributes are called personality. This is what I mean by manifest-Consciousness has attributes.

Prior to Consciousness, or prior to the experience "I am," You existed but were unaware of Your existence. When you began expressing Your Self via manifestation, You assumed attributes. Although these attributes are mistaken to be personal to various bodies, they are the impersonal functioning of Consciousness in Totality. Some people have given this impersonal functioning the name God, others have given It other names.

Names can only be given to something that is experienced. Who you Really are is prior to experiencing, or consciousness.

So, Your manifest "form" may be called Consciousness or God or whatever, but who You Really are is Absolute, non-manifest, and cannot be named or described.

So now you're saying there is something greater than God!
I'm saying that who You really are is beyond concepts. It doesn't matter what name you give the unnamable or what teachings are used to describe It. No concepts, no words, can come near to the Truth because words and concepts can only be used to describe relativity, not Reality.

Relativity signifies relationships between concepts. Reality is beyond concepts and appearances. This means that via the mind—which is limited to conceptualization—you cannot know the Truth. It means that nothing I say is the Truth. Nothing the Bible or anyone else says is the Truth.

All we have in the various teachings are pointers towards That which is indescribable and cannot be talked about. Many of these teachings have become distorted. You cannot be one hundred percent sure of any teachings because they are all colored by the various intellects that put them forward.

All you have to go on is what you sense in your heart. It is fine to listen to what I say, compare it to what you believe, and discard it if you see fit. All I am suggesting is that before you gained all this information about guilt and the need to control, there was peace. Intuitively you know that peace is natural and healthy. Intellectually, you have learned that guilt is necessary, but I am sure it has never felt either natural or healthy to you, has it?

No, it's painful.
And does your heart sense of "God" give you any indication that God is judgmental, cruel, or vindictive?

No.
Your heart sense of "God," if it is in any way similar to what I felt, is full of awe and joy. Now compare that to your intellectual *beliefs* about God and tell me if it compares in any way to what you *feel*.

No, it doesn't.

Your heart sense of God comes from within you. Your beliefs about God have come from outside, from other people. Does the Bible say, "The Kingdom of God is without?" Does the Bible say the Kingdom of God is outside of you?

No. "The Kingdom of God is within."
Don't you think that gives you a fair indication of where to look If you want to know the Truth? Do you think you'll find it in books or in the words of preachers?

No.
And you won't find the Truth here either. All I am giving you here is, perhaps, an alternative to clinging to rigid dogma and external programming. I'm not saying, "This is how it is!" I'm saying, "How can you be sure that what you believe is the Truth?"

It's so painful.
Living life in ignorance of Your Self is painful. That's why teachings worldwide contain the modicum "Know Thyself," and you can't do that if you look for the Truth outside of yourself.

Thank you.

Enlightenment and Other Misconceptions

You want to "attain" enlightenment so that you can feel special. The "one" desiring this special-ness is the only obstruction to realizing that You are not lacking or in need of anything.

Is the newborn child already enlightened?
The term *re-incarnation* is usually used to signify the recurring birth of a particular body or spirit. My sense of this concept is that impersonal Consciousness expresses it-Self via a series of bodyminds. With each bodymind there is the potential for ignorance of Self to end. When, during one of these "lifetimes," prejudice and ignorance fall away the cycle of "re-incarnation" ends. There is no re-birth, so to speak. This would be the case with the Sat-guru who embodies transcendent Consciousness. This means that the newborn infant is potentially ignorant of Self. If this were not the case there would be no "birth". So in that sense no, the newborn infant isn't *enlightened*.
But now put this word *enlightened* into context. It is a concept, a thought. This makes it a prejudice. Paradoxically, the word *enlightened* signifies the absence of prejudice.
Who or what You really are is prior to concepts, prior to prejudice. Does that mean You are enlightened? Is enlightenment anything real?

No. It's just a concept.
You see this concept—*enlightenment*—that people want to

"attain," or own, isn't real. It's just a word. *Enlightenment* doesn't describe the attaining of anything, but the realization that there is nothing to attain.

If you think you own something, you have opinions about that ownership. You think, "this is mine, it doesn't belong to anyone else." That is a strong opinion. Now you want to attain enlightenment, and attaining is all about ownership isn't it? IF you could *attain* enlightenment, own it, wouldn't you have opinions about that?

Yes. Very strong ones! (laughing)

You feel guilt and pride about what you think because you are identified with the mind. You think you *are* the mind. You also think thoughts are personal, which means you think you *own* them. Put the beliefs "I am the mind" and "These are 'my' thoughts" together and you are saying, "I *am* some-thing I own." Ridiculous, eh?

The mind **is** prejudice. It is full of thoughts about *wants* and *not wants*.

The "me" *wants* enlightenment, but enlightenment means the end of *wants*. Do you see the bind you are in?

Yes. It's so ridiculous, but it's so hard to get rid of the mental conditioning. It's so strong.

Recognizing the ridiculousness of the idea of "attaining enlightenment" is the first step. So, you've taken the first step. (laughing)

You can't get rid of conditioning because it happened despite you. It can only cease despite you. You might go to a therapist or do various workshops, and that might look as if it is the cause of the falling away of certain conditioning. But, the decision to undertake these activities also happens despite you. The concept of *cause and effect* simply describes an impersonal synchronicity of events. You don't have any say in this. You don't have a damn thing to do with the unfolding of events. (laughing)

As this understanding deepens habitual thinking patterns begin to unravel. Then gradually, or fast, orientation shifts away from habitual neediness and ideas of attaining, gaining, improving, and becoming.

I feel quite lost sometimes now.
That happens when you start orienting away from your comfort zone. In time you realize that it has never been "comfortable." When habitual ways of acting and interacting stop making sense to you, that feeling of being lost happens. It simply means that the "me" is losing some of its definition.
When you indicate yourself, you point to the heart, not the head – even though you are identified with the mind, which you think is in the head. You point to the heart because the Seat of Consciousness, or manifest Self, is reflected in the Heart center.

But consciousness is throughout the body.
Yes, it is. Are you familiar with the concept of the chakras, or Seats of Consciousness in the body?

Sort of .....
The chakras are a concept that describes the most dynamic energetic manifestations of Consciousness in the body. I won't get into an in-depth explanation of the chakras concept. And do understand that they are just concepts.
It suffices that you understand that they are like the primary dynamos through which Consciousness animates the body. The Heart chakra is the one that balances and *feeds*, as it were, the other centers. We'll call it the primary dynamo.
While the mind is full of rigid prejudice, the animation of the body by Consciousness—via the chakras—is less dynamic. Spontaneity, the nature of Consciousness, appears to be curtailed by the thought, "Actions should, and can, be modified." This means that the chakras are not functioning to their fullest potential. The chakras are always depicted as being separate to each other, but when ignorance falls away this is no longer the case. This is because the system is functioning to its fullest potential.
The Heart chakra is the balancing center of the other chakras.

85

This means that when the mind and prejudicial thoughts are identified with, the Heart center is rarely felt. This is why—in some teachings—it is said that the mind is the "covering" of the Heart.

When manifestation—possessions, religion, and other people—fail to satisfy you anymore, you experience feeling empty. If this emptiness becomes a strong enough feeling, the question "Who am I?" may arise. This is how seeking often begins.

And even more frustration and emptiness! (laughing)
If seeking is undertaken with the idea you'll "attain," then for sure you'll only find frustration. That's because the "covering" of mind is just getting stronger. The person you think you are is just adding more layers of ego-armor.

If seeking is one-pointed and undertaken with the understanding that what you seek isn't missing, then it also gets frustrating. Actually, my experience was less of frustration and more of a growing sense of confusion and heartache.

This is all that needs to happen, that Consciousness, or "I Amness," orients more and more towards the Heart. When the yearning to know Self, or the Divine, becomes strong enough, it does all the work from then on. The mind just turns increasingly inward, and previous fixations about the external world hold less and less interest for you.

The deeper the understanding goes, that Self is not any-thing to be attained, the more the mind reflects this in confusion. When this confusion is *total*, the mind reflects this in the thought "I can *never* understand or know Self." In that moment, the seeking stops and the misperceptions begin to fall away. But, you have to reach the point where you totally give up trying to understand before this can happen.

Void of rigid prejudices, the "covering" of the Heart subsides. At first this results in the experiencing of tremendous joy, love, and gratitude.

The mind is absent of worry and fear and this gives the experience of such ecstasy. You know how it is when you feel wonderful; you don't care and don't feel strong prejudice towards

86

anything—nothing matters.

If the feelings of ecstasy aren't interpreted as "I have attained," the "covering" of the Heart won't re-establish itself.

But you experienced emptiness or depression before this happened?

Yes, for two years beforehand and briefly afterwards too.

The habit of identities kept me stuck in believing that what I was looking for would feel like an identity. It took a while to realize that Self is the subtlest of subtlests. I'd spent my whole life filling the emptiness with identities, and when they started to fall away, the mind turned in circles booting up interpretations about this *emptiness*.

It took a while to realize that Self didn't feel like an identity at all, but was the absence of them. It's not that I don't still identify *with* roles, age, gender, etc., but I don't think of myself as *being* them.

Because I still experienced "Esther" with her personality, body, and mind, I thought the Self was still not "realized." I really hadn't understood that it was simply a matter of realizing that she was not Me.

It took a while before I figured out that identification *as* and identification *with* are very different. Relatively speaking, when identification *as* subsides, there is a huge difference because guilt and fear just fall away. But because I was still identified *with*, I was confused.

Until the pseudo-self was recognized as false, I misunderstood experiencing to be caused by the body. That sounds so ridiculous to me now that it's impossible to believe I ever thought that way.

When I stopped thinking of myself as some-body, I was still expecting Self to feel like an identity. It took a while for me to understand that my essential nature, or Self, IS *experiencing*. It's only then that I realized that there was a huge difference between identifying *as* the bodymind, and identifying *with* it.

Thank you. That helped a lot.

That there is still identification *with* the "I" or personality means the process is incomplete. The *intellect* relates to the concepts of "I" and "mine." Even though I know there is no such thing as personal ownership and that I am not this "I," this knowing is happening in relation to the story of Esther.

Because the knowing—I am not Esther—is centered around her, it means the mind is still colored by her particular personality. Although there aren't any rigid prejudices anymore one can't say prejudice is absent. This is because all thoughts are judgments and, therefore, prejudice.

Only when the "I" or intellect and identification *with* ceases, is prejudice absolutely absent. That is the final stage in the relative process, that all prejudice ceases. And this can only happen when Esther is fully out of the picture.

Can you explain a bit more?
I know there is no real difference between me and others, and that there are no "others," other than in relative terms. However, as long as Esther figures in the picture, there are still thoughts about her in relation to others. That is the paradox: the knowing is that there are no "others," but there are still thoughts about "Esther" in relation to "others."

Only when the experience of duality ceases being centered around a dualistic "I" is there direct Knowledge of the unfolding of duality within the non-dual Self. At the moment, one could say my understanding is still indirect. It is an intuiting of the whole picture, but because Esther still figures in the picture there is not total objectivity about it.

Total objectivity can only happen when prejudice is absent. That thoughts are no longer rigid ideals is a tremendous difference, relatively speaking. From the perspective of people around me this difference is often felt very strongly because it is a big contrast to their own experience of self.

I know that relativity has no bearing on Reality; on Me. However, until the relative process is complete there is only indirect knowing happening via the body called "Esther."

How does it complete?
My understanding is that the relative process reaches completion only in rare cases. IF it completes while the body is still around, this completion is preceded by the deepening of dispassion or impartiality. The love of being is very strong, and the habit of intellect is very strong. The thoughts "I" and "mine" are the biggest habit. Before they can subside there has to be total dispassion towards the consciousness.

What do you mean, "total dispassion towards the consciousness"?
Another word for consciousness is *knowing* (and not-knowing in dreamless sleep).
Right now, the knowing happening via your body is being misinterpreted. The knowing happening via my body is clearly understood. I know that My essential nature, or Self, *is* this *knowing* or *experiencing*. You think you are a bodymind, which knows something. I know that I am no-body and that via the mind I can have no understanding of the Truth.
In the stage from ajnani (ignorance of Self) to jnani (Knowing) the sense "I know nothing," has to reach a point where it feels so overwhelming that the need to understand just falls away. In the absence of any thought about "I can understand," and in the absence of need or yearning, in that moment the misperception of Self begins to fall into perspective.
Once the knowing of who You are not is quite clear, then it is almost as if a replay of this whole process happens. The undistorted knowing that is embodied in jnani is still not direct Knowledge, so to speak. This is because the experience of duality is being filtered through the mind. If this is understood, and it often isn't, the mind starts booting up questions.
Because there is indirect knowing of Self, rather than *direct* Knowledge, questions arise. Because there are questions, my sense is that there is still a residual trace of "I can understand." After all, the function of the mind is *understanding* and *conceptualizing*. This is why, while duality is known via the mind, perception is still colored by a trace of prejudice, a trace

89

of "I can understand."

Questions come, but they are clearly understood to be a deepening of discrimination. It isn't that answers are sought, but that the questions themselves put the knowing into a clearer and clearer perspective. And that perspective is that the process is incomplete.

The realization deepens that via the mind there is only intuiting of My True nature. As this realization deepens so does dispassion towards this consciousness, which *is* the *intuiting* of My True nature. Only when dispassion or impartiality is total towards this consciousness or "I" does it cease being the medium via which I indirectly know about My True nature.

But you know You are That?

I know I am not this consciousness, which will end with the death of the body. I know I am That which precedes and gives rise to this consciousness, yes. But this knowing is not objective because it is happening in relation to the "I" or unique personality called Esther.

Only when Esther is fully out of the picture will knowing subside into objective Knowledge. When, or if, the intermediary of Esther ceases being identified *with*, only then will knowing subside. My perspective on duality would then no longer be an indirect perspective happening via one particular aspect of duality.

You, the Absolute, precede knowing and not-knowing. When you realize You aren't an object-identity, the knowing of Self loses its distortions. However, at this stage you only know who You are not, and this knowing happens via the object that has now fallen into clearer perspective. You intuit that you are That which precedes this consciousness but, while "I-consciousness" is still central to your experience, one can only say you intuit Your True nature. You intuit "I am That."

When "I-consciousness" subsides, so does knowing or intuiting. Your perception of the world could be said to be more objective, but because it is happening via a particular object it is still quasi-subjective. Only when identification with this body-object ceases and the "I" subsides is there total objectivity.

90

Relatively speaking, the embodiment of this Objectivity or Knowledge is termed Sat-guru or the highest "level" of jnani. The Sat-guru embodies the non-dual Absolute "within" duality. In Sat-guru even identification *with* the body has ceased. This means that prejudice is absent and so it is only the Sat-guru that can be considered to be the embodiment of full enlightenment. But remember, *enlightenment* describes a relative difference only.

Then there is no re-birth. I mean there's no re-birth in the sense you were talking about re-incarnation.
No there isn't.
Your only concern while you have a body is to become fully conversant with this "I am-consciousness." Right now, you know it through distortions. First you have to be totally convinced that You are NOT these distortions.

It seems so simple and yet so hard! (sigh)
Your existence is like a riddle. The source of this riddle Is the solution. The reverse reflection of this source IS knowing and not-knowing.

I don't get it.
If you did, you wouldn't be here. (laughing)
When you are in deep dreamless sleep we can call that not-knowing. You are unaware of yourself. When you wake up, retrospectively you know about this.
Knowing and not-knowing are Your essential, manifest nature. Prior to knowing and not-knowing You are, but unaware of Your Self. When the body appeared and the mind linked the sense "I am" to the body, the misinterpretation arose that "I am some-body."
The reversal of this process happens when you begin to realize that You are not the body and that the body isn't the cause of consciousness or experiencing.
Do you think the body is self-animating; that it is the cause of consciousness?

It can only be the other way round. The body can't animate
consciousness.
Consciousness *is* the animation of the body. Without
consciousness the body is deemed "dead." In the same way a
machine doesn't animate electricity the body can't animate
consciousness.
The body cannot be the animator of itself. Without
Consciousness the body is just an inanimate object. It has
always been an inanimate object. It is an inanimate object filled
with animation. The body cannot BE that animation. Do you see
that?

Yes.
First, there is no-thingness or the absence of phenomena. The
body appears out of no-thingness. Out of no-thingness, the
appearance of some-thing has arisen. The *presence* of the body
is contrasted against the *absence* of phenomena.
The contrast between the body and Awareness registers in the
mind as the thought "I Am."
The word *mind* describes a collection of thoughts and images.
In the absence of things, where would the mind be?

It wouldn't.
In the absence of the body and the rest of manifestation, there
would be nothing to think about. There would also be no
medium through which that thinking could happen. The mind
has a beginning and an end. You don't cause the mind to come
into effect, and you don't cause consciousness to start animating
the bodymind.
You know that consciousness and the mind came about with
your "birth," and it's clear you had no say in that "birth."
If you think about this just a little, you'll realize that
consciousness and the mind happened despite you. This means
that you began life out of control of both of these concepts.
Once you understand this, you'll begin to realize that the idea
that you now have control is ludicrous. How could
consciousness and the mind, which have given rise to the sense

"I am," come about beyond your control and then suddenly come under your control?

They can't.
This is the first understanding you have to come to before the reversal of the misperception of Self—as some-one with personal power—can fall away.
Then you have to realize that self-consciousness is dependant on a bodymind that has a beginning and an end. This means that self-consciousness has a beginning and an end. If you are something that has a beginning and an end it means you don't exist, because *existence* describes undoubted presence. *Existence* doesn't describe something that's here today and gone tomorrow.

What do you mean? Something can exist today and be destroyed tomorrow?
How can you be sure that the car you saw in front of your house yesterday was really there? Perhaps it was a figment of your imagination. Perhaps you were hallucinating. You can't be sure, and you can't say the car that was there yesterday *definitely* existed.
You know that the mind is capable of all kinds of imaginings and hallucinations, so you can't be one hundred percent sure that something you see now and not later ever existed.

Okay, I see that.
The only existence you have never doubted for a moment is your own. You haven't needed anyone to tell you that you exist and you don't need to prove it to anyone. You've mistaken this sense of *being* and interpreted it to mean you are an object, but still, you know you exist.
While you know "I am," you question all kinds of phenomena, but few question how they know about themselves.
While you have a body your only concern is to get to know this animation, this "I amness," as well as you possibly can. Right now you have only a distorted image of it. You focus on your

object-identity and don't think to ask how the experiencing of anything is possible.

How do we "get to know" consciousness? What do you mean exactly?
In the times when you "lose yourself" in an activity, actions happen spontaneously and efficiently. You know, like when you drive from A to B and then don't know how you got there. Or when you paint a picture or do anything you deeply enjoy—in those times that you lose yourself, there is peace. You only know about it retrospectively, but you know there was effortlessness.
Pay attention to such times because they will tell you a lot about this consciousness. Minus thoughts of you-the-bodymind—minus the false self—this animating principle or Consciousness functions very dynamically. Actions are spontaneous, uninhibited, and effortless.
If you want to know Consciousness for what it is, go play more; do the things that absorb you easily.

I like that recipe! (laughing)
Mmm, well we'll wait and see if you use it! For a lot of people *play* seems way too easy. Abstinence might sound like a more virtuous recipe! (laughing)
While the delusion "I am some-body" persists, most actions *seem* like efforts. That's why people enjoy playtime and goofing-off, because that's the only time they forget themselves—forget the false self.
What you need to understand is that, even though you think you have control over actions, even seemingly controlled actions still happen spontaneously. Even actions that look like personal efforts are spontaneous.

When the body dies and consciousness ends, is there the awareness of being absent?
You do the math. (laughing) Did you know about yourself before the "birth" of the body?

94

I don't know. I only know what happened once the body was born.
And you learned about your "birth" from your parents, yes?

Yes.
Did your Mum or Dad need to tell you, "You exist" before you could experience being present?

No.
Your "birth" is something you learned about. "Death" is something you have learned about. You also learned, "I am this and that." But before you *learned* all this, you knew you were. Before you *learned* about your existence, the sense of presence was already there.
So, has everything you've learned in your lifetime helped you know the Truth of You? Has anything you've learned given you lasting peace?

No, hardly. I don't know who I am. I thought, "I know who I am!" before I started coming here. Now that I sit listening to you, I realize I haven't got a clue. (laughing)
Ah, but you do have a clue! You have the only clue you need, but you've been ignoring it. You know "I am," and that is the clue to knowing Your Self.
You're like someone who has money in the bank and lives off scraps, lamenting his sad condition. You look at your check-book register and blame yourself for all the debits. You look at all the credits and congratulate yourself. All your focus is on the past balances and what you hope to gain in the future. Meanwhile, you don't bother to look at how much collateral you actually have "in hand."
This is exactly how you are when it comes to your perception of self. Your mind contains the information "I am"—one could say that is the balance you have "in hand." But you ignore what is and focus on what was, what you *want* to become, who you *think* you should be, and who you *think* you are. This leads to

all kinds of misery, guilt, and fear. You are living on assumptions.

I'm telling you that who You are is not a debit, is not missing or lacking in any way. You also can't be *more* than You are. But you focus on what you were, what you think you are, what you hope to become. You focus on what was, what is not, and what might be. As long as that carries on, all you know is what *seems* to be, not what Is.

You already are, and you know that you *are*. Until now you thought you were some-body. Now you are beginning to see that this is a faulty perception. So you ask the question "Who am I?" and it seems that the answer to this question is never going to come to you. And you are right, because You are the source of the question and the one wanting answers is nothing more than a reverse reflection of this source.

What do you mean?
Can a reflection turn around and see itself or know about itself?

No.
You stand in front of the mirror and see your body. You know it isn't anyone else's body. Right now you see the reflection of your body in duality and think you *are* it. That is as ridiculous as thinking that the reflection of your body in the mirror is you. The mind is like a mirror in which Consciousness is reflected in the words "I am." For many years my mind linked the bodymind called Esther to this sense of presence and I mistook myself to BE the body. Now the mind has ceased offering up this distorted reflection and I know I am not any-body. However, as long as the mirror of mind is being used, this knowing—however clear it may be compared to before—is an indirect experience of manifest-Self or impersonal Consciousness.

I know that Consciousness is the impersonal functioning happening through my and other bodies. But as long as this knowing is centered around one particular body, which I call "mine," my perspective on the impersonality of Consciousness isn't absolutely objective.

But you know it's impersonal.
Yes, but I know this via a personal body and so my perspective is not fully objective. That is the paradox, that I know I am not any appearance, but I know this *via* an appearance. This means that the mind still serves as an intermediary or mirror via which I know about Self.

When, or if, the mind ceases reflecting this personality called Esther, my perspective will be totally objective: from the standpoint of the Subject. Of course, that has always been the case, but until duality ceases being experienced via the mirror of Esther's particular mind and intellect, I only intuit my True nature. I have no doubts about it but cannot say there is *direct* Knowledge.

Right now there is *knowing* and it is indirect because the mirror of mind is still being used as a medium. The next stage is that the "mirror" subsides and this may or may not happen during the "life" of the body.

As dispassion or impartiality grows, it grows even towards this consciousness or "I." When dispassion is total the mind becomes, so to speak, transparent. All prejudice, all thoughts, subside, including the knowing of "I."

When the knowing "I" ceases being reflected in the mind it means that the unique intellect has subsided. The "mirror" is gone. Then there is absolute objective Knowledge.

Prior to questioning, prior to learning, prior to Consciousness, and all the labels that have been added to it, You are. You are the source of the question "Who am I?" If You did not exist, the question would not arise. It couldn't be asked if You didn't exist. This means that You are both the source of questioning and, as such, You are also the *answer.*

The first step is to recognize that the reflection the mind is giving you is distorted. By means of the mind you can begin to understand this, and that is the paradox. You can use the mind to unravel itself.

Right now it feels like one big jumbled knot.

At least that means your mind is no longer full of neat sets of ideals and beliefs about, "This is how it is!" That's a beginning. First you have to "get" that nothing you know about yourself is the truth. Then you start trying to figure the truth out and find it's impossible. The more deeply you understand this, the more you realize "I know nothing." That's when the unraveling process really gets underway.

But you are already clear on this?
I am much clearer on this. The paradox is that when this *clarity* happens the mind boots starts booting up more information than ever. It is full of thoughts about this new perspective on Self. That is why, even at the jnani stage, there needs to be intense discrimination. Perspective needs to be kept very clear on all this, otherwise the relative process is unlikely to come to completion.
Until the illusory self or "I" totally disappears from the picture discrimination must continue. The addiction to intellect and the love of being is so strong that unless perspective is kept on all this the "I" is unlikely to subside. When it does, then the relative process completes.
This is a description of the relative process of what is termed *enlightenment*. Light is being shed on the ignorance of Self. If discrimination continues, the mind orients further and further away from the illusion. Then, in certain cases, the light of Consciousness dispels all ignorance and thought-prejudice. That would be what is called *full enlightenment*, which is merely a term that describes a relative difference in perspective. A huge difference, but only from the standpoint of the relative. *Enlightenment* is nothing real. It has no bearing on Reality.

What? You haven't attained
Enlightenment yet?
Try harder!
Try harder!
You know all riddles
Can be solved.

Why ask me about your
Destiny?
How would I know your purpose?
I never left home,
Or did anything
Worthwhile.

I have never been a mystery
To my-Self, because
I know that, "I Am."
That is the only proof
I need, this Knowing

EV

You say you once had control.
How did you lose it?
What's that you say?
You have no control
Over control!

You say you create your own reality.
So you are omnipotent?!
What's that you say?
Everyone creates
Their own reality!

EV

Control and Purpose

**If control were really possible, would the desiring of it still
be there?
If control were really possible, would you still fear the lack
of it?**

*It seems most people are content to muddle along and cope with
life as best they can. You know, it just seems most people are
happy just coping with what is and not questioning deeper.*

If they were really content, they wouldn't be slaves to *shoulds*
and *should nots*. If they were really content, they wouldn't ever
think in terms of coping. Coping is all about partial living and
quasi control. It certainly doesn't describe a state of contentment.
But yes, some people are more content than others. They may
never question further. In your case, you are here, and that tells
me a spark of discontent, or at least curiosity, is there. Perhaps
this spark will grow into a fire, perhaps not. It doesn't really
matter, because it's all just a pastime.

Who You really are, already IS. Who You really are doesn't need
anything. But *your* experience is one of need. You want to know
the Truth about Your Self. For this to happen, you must first
deeply understand the personal lie. You must be absolutely clear
as to who You are NOT. The Principle behind the story of "you"
preceded this story. This "I amness" is nothing more than an
impermanent appearance upon the backdrop of the Eternal, unchanging Principle—and You *are* That.

First you must become totally familiar with this "I amness." You
have to understand what it is minus all the trappings of identities—body, mind, gender, and name, etc. To know this "I amness"
minus words and material identities is to BE beyond it. You al-

101

ready *are* beyond this consciousness, but that is not the experience right now.

Recognize that you cannot BE anything you perceive. Perception of anything necessitates separateness from it. You have the perception of this "I amness." That is your experience now, although it is clouded by all the trappings and labels. See the labels for what they are—something separate to You and impermanent. When this understanding is total you will have an undistorted experience of this "I amness." The Ultimate "step," is beyond knowing and not-knowing.

Phew, I just can't make any sense out of this now.
The five senses, the body, and the mind, and this "I amness" are the flowering of the Ultimate principle. You are That, but until you see the mirage of this "me" for what it is, you flounder around, bouncing between concepts. You stay a slave to concepts and think you can, and need to, maintain control over them.

This belief in control gives you the idea that the pseudo-you can "attain" knowledge of the Self. In this quest, most seekers fall in the trap of believing that the body and mind are obstacles to the search.

As long as they believe that the body and mind are something to be rejected, they are rather like someone who is dying of thirst in the middle of a pool of spring water. Rather than just drinking the water they think, "I just need the wetness, not the water." In believing, this they stay there, dying of thirst, vainly trying to extract the wetness.

Can you explain that a bit more?
What do you consider the obstacle to knowing who You really are?

It still feels as if it's the mind.
Just being human. This humanness feels like the obstacle. (laughing)
Yes, that was my big hurdle. I was sure my humanness was the obstacle. Then, when I met Ramesh, what struck me so deeply

was that he appeared so human. There was absolutely nothing guru-like about him. He acted in a very straightforward way, with such a sense of humor and gentleness. In those first days with Ramesh I began to realize that my humanness couldn't possibly be an obstacle. Prior to meeting him I sort of understood this, but my humanness and my beliefs about it always seemed to get in the way.

Understand that the mind and the body, which make up what you call "humanness," are the mechanisms that make the experience of *being* possible. Without them, how would you know "I am"?

But, if we aren't the mind or the body, they are blinding us to who we Are, aren't they?

What's "blinding" you is the belief that you *are* the mind and body. You have spent your life thinking, "This is how it is!" You have taken these beliefs to be absolute truths. This rigid opinion about pseudo-truths is the obstacle to knowing the real Truth. You know about this pseudo-identity via the mind. You have thoughts about seeking the Self via the mind. Without the body and mind there would be no seeking happening, would there?

I see that.

You seek the Self via the mechanisms of mind and body. All the while you think the mind and body are obstacles to seeking. So you try to reject the mind, and maybe penalize the body with fasting and rigid exercises. This is no less ridiculous than someone "dying" of dehydration, thinking he has first to extract the wetness from water before he can satiate his thirst.

Wetness is the essential nature of water. In this same way, *beingness* is the essential nature, the essence of the body. How do you think you can know your essential nature by getting rid of the body and mind? How can the body be an obstacle to knowing its essence? That would be like trying to taste the sweetness of sugar without biting into the sugar lump.

How can the mind, which gives you data on this essence, be an obstacle? Even if the data is a misinterpretation right now, it is this data that has set you seeking. Frustration, with all the mental data on "you," has led to this search. Now you are using the capacity of thinking to unravel thoughts.

Both the body and mind are necessary for the taste of "I amness" to be possible. The essence of the body is "I amness." The experiencing of this "I amness" happens because the mind is informing you about it in thoughts. So, rejecting the body and mind in order to know the Self is like "throwing the baby out with the bathwater," as Nisargadatta used to say.

Why did the body and mind appear in the first place?
When you do something spontaneously you usually do so because of "no particular reason." You don't give reasons for your actions—you just act. The appearance of the body and mind happened in the same way—spontaneously, for no particular reason. Most people spend their lives looking for a reason. Some think they discover their reason for *being* by finding their life's purpose. When this is the case, at the moment of "death," what has that purpose served?

They feel they haven't lived their lives in vain.
Life as they know it is about to end. They are about to lose the sense "I am," and when it's gone who has gained anything from having a purpose?

While they were alive they probably felt better about themselves.
Yes, they probably did feel better about having a purpose. But what use is the purpose to them the moment this consciousness ceases animating the body?

They probably feel they benefited others. They leave a legacy behind perhaps.
But how does that benefit *them*?
Let's say that you find your life's purpose today. Tomorrow you are paralyzed from the neck down and can't do anything. You can't even talk or move your little finger. What use is that life's purpose then?

It isn't any use.
To find your life's purpose may help you to cope and feel better about yourself. But if you are unable to then carry out that purpose, you discover your dependency on it. You discover that it helped you feel in control. Don't you think that is what finding a purpose is all about—control?

Yes. Yes, I can see that feeling useful and as if my life has a reason helps me feel in control.
The feeling of control is dependent on the receptivity of others and on what situations occur in your life. The feeling of control is dependent on you having a healthy body and a coherently functioning mind—even if it is absent of logic much of the time. (laughing)
A lot of people think their life's purpose is to be purveyors of fundamental, rigid beliefs. This has nothing to do with clear reasoning and everything to do with rigid programming.
Fundamental, dogmatic beliefs are always underlain by doubt. This is why such people need others to validate their beliefs—although, they aren't necessarily aware of the motive behind their pontificating.

Wouldn't you say that you are fairly strong in your statements?
Yes, my statements are very strong, but have I once told you that you *have* to believe what I'm telling you? I keep on asking you to investigate for yourselves, not to take what I say as gospel truth. These statements come spontaneously, void of agenda, so their strength isn't needy of your receptivity. Although at times I do just want to scream and shake you and say, "It's so simple, don't you see!"

Isn't that involvement?
If you are here, it is because Self is ready to commune with Self. You may still see me as the personality "Esther," and you may come here as the personality Amy or Mark; but what happens here is beyond these personalities. If you understand this, it will be that much easier for you.
When you come here there is communing of Self with the Self. If

the sense to shake and scream at you arises, it is mirroring your own frustrations, that's all. Unfortunately, the complacency and lethargy of coping has put many of you so out of touch with this frustration that it requires a strong mirror before you realize it's even there. I provide this mirroring of your frustrations. Isn't that nice of me. (laughing)

Yes, thanks a lot! (laughing) *I certainly know frustration is there, and it just seems to grow.*
Good. When there is frustration it's impossible to be complacent. Welcome the frustration because it means that coping isn't enough for you anymore. Coping and complacency aren't enough for you any more.
Here I serve as a reflection only. Sometimes you glimpse beyond the personality and the mind quiets and you experience peace. Sometimes you bang up against the reflection because you are thinking in terms of me as a personality and yourself as a personality. Then you experience confusion and frustration. These experiences are nothing more than a mirroring of both Your essential nature and your distorted sense of it. When you experience confusion, you want to control it and it doesn't feel good. When you experience peace, there is no thought of control.

But even though we get those glimpses of peace, the desire for control doesn't go away—not for very long anyway.
No, but perhaps control will gradually make less and less sense to you. Since you have spent most of your life trying to control, there has to be some benefit to it, don't you think? It would be strange to desire something that doesn't benefit you.

Well, there doesn't seem to be any benefit. It just seems to bring more and more neediness.
There has to be some idea of benefit or you wouldn't be so addicted to control, would you? What you have to do is question your beliefs about control. You have had them all your life, so now investigate what is so beneficial, so *important* about having control. (laughing)

I don't know, but there is fear when I think about not having it.
Have you ever really had control? And IF you had control, why
did you let go of it? After all, *control* means the ability to restrain
and command. IF you have that ability, it seems to me that control can't be anything partial. Either you have control or you don't.
Once you have it, are you saying you don't have control over
maintaining control?

Can you explain that some more? I didn't quite get what you said.
Control means the ability to command or restrain. As control can
disappear at any moment, it means you really don't have the
ability to restrain or command anything, doesn't it?

Well, temporarily we can have control.
Listen to what you are saying! In essence you are saying, "Control is an absolute until it isn't." That's like saying truth is an
absolute until it's a lie, or freedom is an absolute until it is limitation. Within the relative experience there are no absolutes. The
word *absolute* means unconditional, perfect, and unlimited. Now,
if control is real, it has to be unconditional, perfect, and unlimited. It can't be here one moment and gone the next. Do you see
that?

Yes, but it's so confusing.
You see, the mind has been trundling along on the same track all
your life. The mind holds information and holds only superficial
questions about that information. The information you like, you
adopt; the information you dislike, you try to ignore. Unfortunately, the first bit of information you learned was "I am some-
body." With the adoption of this bit of information as an *absolute
truth*, the whole problem began. Everyone adopts the information "I am some-body" unquestioningly. As a result the need to
control the body and the mind and all other objects results. Because you believe other bodies can affect your body and because
you think You are this body, you spend all your time trying to
control the bodies around you.

107

To see beyond this false identity, you have to find a way of recognizing that the combination of the body, the mind, and "I am-consciousness," that you call "me," is an illusion—a faulty perception.

But how can we do that?
That is what is happening here. Your minds are being stimulated to boot up tangential thoughts. When your minds are thrown off-track, confused thoughts are the result. Then you feel more out of control than when you arrived here.

YOU have never been, nor have you ever needed to be, in control. The mind contains out of control, confused thoughts; however, You are NOT the mind. Whether you know it or not, that is why you are here, to lose this idea of control. To realize that control is a myth, an illusion. One of the easiest ways this is going to happen is if you are forced to re-evaluate all the personal truths you have held until now.

Tonight we are investigating concepts that you have been buying into all your life—the concept of control and the idea that you exist as a "thing." You have spent your entire life believing "I am some-body," and "I exist as such." But now, perhaps, you understand that this inconstant, ever-changing "me" cannot be said to exist.

The word *exist* describes a constant, unchanging, indisputable presence. IF you are the body and mind, and this pseudo-self is a fact, a truth—what will happen the minute the body is proclaimed "dead"? Mustn't the fact, the truth of *you-the-bodymind* be considered an untruth?

Well, the bodymind exists and then ceases to exist.
IF this pseudo-you is a truth today and no longer a truth tomorrow, can you say it was ever a truth?

No. Well, it was a relative truth.
Yes, a "relative truth," and relative truths are never absolutes. *Relative* signifies in relation to something else. What does this truth, "I am the bodymind," relate to?

The body while it exists?
Listen again. Existence means *irrefutable fact*, or *presence that cannot be doubted*. If something is present one moment and absent the next, doesn't it mean the absence was already in potential in the presence?

Yes. So it's paradox.
It's all paradox. And paradox means a self-contradictory statement. In other words, paradox describes a concept that also contains its contradiction. So, one could say that a concept is both what it is and what it is not. What does this mean to you?

I can't get my mind around it.
Exactly, you can't get your mind around it because the mind *is* the language of concepts, and all concepts contain both the presence and absence of themselves. The concept of peace is only possible because you know about the concept of strife. If you only knew about peace, would there be any thought of struggle or control? If you only knew about freedom and knew nothing of limitation, would there be any desire for freedom? No concepts would exist unless they had something to be compared to, would they? Think about it.

But then you are saying concepts do exist?
If concepts are *really* juxtaposed opposites that have nothing to do with one-another, one must consider them absolutes. If this is the case, then yes, concepts exist and are real. But now you tell me of one concept that *exists* minus any other concept to compare it to. Give me one concept that stands alone and has no opposite.

There aren't any.
That means the minute you think about one concept it is because you believe it's opposite also exists. Can you come up with any concept at all without simultaneously acknowledging its contradiction?

No.
When you really "get" this deeply you will realize that you are not, and have never been, a concept, a "thing." The concept of "thing-ness" is only possible because you know about "no-thing-ness."
First there has to be space before you can put something in it, no? Before this accumulation of identities happened there was just the sense of being—this "I amness." For that sense of presence to appear, there had first to be space, or absence, in which it could arise.
Would you say that this sense of presence is dependent on absence?

Yes, when you put it like that, that's what I'd have to say. I guess presence, like any other concept, contains absence.
Don't guess! I'm asking you what you think. I'm not saying, "This is how it is!" People have told you, "This is how it is," since you were a child. I'm not doing that. I'm asking you to come up with your own answer. Do you really think presence can contain absence?

As far as I can figure it out there has to be absence before there can be presence. There has to be space before anything can be put in it.
Absence, or space, or no-thingness, would have to precede thing-ness. So, thing-ness can't contain no-thingness. It has to be the other way round.

Well an empty vase contains nothing.
Can a vase *contain* nothing? Surely there has to be space or no-thing-ness around the vase, and if that no-thingness is also "in" the vase can you really say the vase *contains* nothing? It is surrounded, inside and outside, by nothing.

Ah, I see what you mean.
And what might come before no-thingness?

I don't know. There is nothing that could come before it as far as I can see.
Doesn't that mean that absence, or no-thingness, is an absolute?

Well, it isn't always no-thingness if things appear in it.
Could you know about the concept of *nothing* if you didn't have the concept of *something* to compare it to?

No, I couldn't.
Now go back to basics. How is the knowing of either concept—no-thingness or thing-ness—possible?

Because I have a mind!
Because you "have" a mind! Not because you "are" the mind. Do you see that? You can't BE something you say you own.
The mind is the vehicle via which you know "I am." Now use the mind constructively. Find out how this knowing is possible. Something had to precede this knowing, this experience of being. So what was it? Who were you prior to the "birth" of the body?

My mind doesn't have any answers for that.
Exactly. The mind contains no solutions as to who you were prior to "birth." The mind reflects *beliefs* about no-thingness, but it has never contained any information on no-thingness. The mind boots up terrifying thoughts about no-thingness and contains ideas about heaven and the after-life. This is how you cope with the idea of no-thingness.
In some teachings, the concept of no-thingness is referred to as the Void. But you don't know for sure that these concepts are real. You have never seen them—just heard about them. You have never experienced no-thingness because you have always known "I am" in relation to *things*. Will you ever experience the disappearance of your sense of presence?

No, I can't imagine I will.
Do you have any recall of the beginning of experiencing being? Do you know the exact moment it started?

No.

All you have to go on is what you know—this experience of being. That is where you must begin your investigation, because it is the only clue you have to begin solving the mystery of You. Being a child, being a teenager, being an adult have all been experiences. They were only possible because you experience being. You've struggled with each of these stages, adapting to the new identities. But this struggle and the perception of these identities wouldn't be possible if you didn't first know "I am."

Because the only constant you have ever known is this sense of presence, this "I amness," it's your only collateral. This consciousness, or sense of presence, is the only clue you have that hasn't undergone any change during your life experience. You think "you" have changed, but the sense of presence has never changed, even if it has seemed to be colored by various events.

Those colorful experiences haven't changed the experience of being in any way. You think, "Now I am sad," "Now I am happy," but you can only have these perceptions because you experience being. The experience of being has never stopped during waking and dreaming states. So begin with that experience. Investigate it fully and find out how it began. Any sense of presence has to be preceded by absence. This means that absence is an absolute and, therefore, Eternal.

But presence comes about and appeared in the absence.

If something "comes about," it means that at some time it wasn't there, doesn't it?

This means that presence is temporal; it relates to time. Time is a concept that has come about in relation to space and the objects that appear in it. Without objects, where would there be any sense of time or space? You can only talk about space because you relate it to the distance between objects. So space is another concept that has only come about because of objects. *Space* describes the distance or measurement between objects. Of course people think of space as being an absolute, like all other concepts. Physicists will tell you that you are basically empty space.

What they mean is that *you are an object and it is actually empty space.*

A concept is a "thing," however ephemeral or illusive the "thing" is it's describing. By saying you are not an object and that you are just empty space, the physicist is simply offering you another concept to identify with. But, of course, you can't identify with empty space because you experience existing and you think *existence* signifies something tangible or perceptible. Have you ever had the experience of empty space?

Yes, when I was out in the desert.
But there is something below you and something beyond the desert. So you can only experience partial space, isn't that so? Space, as you know it, is never absolutely empty. For a start, to experience space, the body is necessary, isn't it? As the body is there *in space*—even if it's floating outside of a space ship—you can't say you experience absolute space.

Physicists have proven that no-thing exists and the only explanation they can come up with is that all there is, is empty space or Consciousness. Right now, probably more physicists prefer the *empty-space theory.* But it still doesn't give the physicist an absolute answer to existence. This is because the physicist, like anyone else, is limited by the fact that the mind can only come up with concepts, which are never absolutes.

My mind is exhausted just thinking about it all. It makes me realize I know absolutely nothing, and that I can never know anything.
This realization is all that has to happen. Perhaps it is just beginning to dawn on you that you know *absolutely* nothing about the Truth. (laughing) Perhaps this realization is just an inkling or an intellectual understanding. But, as this understanding goes deeper, the frustration grows. The mind turns in circles and you almost give up searching, and then you try a bit more. If the frustration goes deep enough that is all that is required. You have to be convinced that you cannot know the Truth, that, via the mind, you cannot know an absolute. You have to be convinced that you have *absolutely* no control over anything. The instant you give up

trying to understand is the instant your whole perspective on Self changes.

So it seems that it has to be painful? It has to be frustrating and confusing and it feels totally depressing.
Unfortunately, this does seem to be the case. In most cases one has to "hit a wall," as they say, before giving up is total. And before that happens, you just feel like you're bouncing off the wall much of the time. (laughing)

It's so scary though.
Well, you have the *apparent* choice of continuing to live a life struggling for control or facing your greatest fear—that you have no control. Unfortunately, you have no say, no control, over this decision. If the mind had any control, or was self-animating, it might take the plunge and go for it, but the mind is an accumulation of concepts, so to let go of concepts is impossible for it. This would mean letting go of itself.

 If you had control, you might take the plunge and let go of control, but because you think you are an object with control, that would mean letting go of *you*. Obviously you can't let go of you. Just understanding this shows you that you have no control over yourself. Everything has always happened despite you. What has to happen is that you become exhausted trying to understand Your Self. The accumulation of concepts and the identification with this accumulation began despite you. If the misperception ceases, it might look as if meditation or something else triggered the cessation. Whatever precedes the cessation of the misperception is just part of the synchronicity of events. It isn't going to cease because of anything you do or don't do. You really don't have any say in it either way.

So we can but hope.
Actually, hope is the "problem." Hope is the coping mechanism that your life has been based upon until now. There is really no difference between hope and coping. As long as the belief in control is there, hope goes hand in hand with it. When the mind

is void of *all* thoughts about hope and the ability to understand, only then does the misperception begin falling away.

Whatever your present experience, it is all you know and it cannot be avoided. You can struggle to change it. You can effort to improve it. But the experience is still what it is, an experience. You can't avoid experiencing because *experiencing* IS Your essential nature.

You might begin experiencing life more fully as this understanding goes deeper. And you might find resistance surfacing towards certain experiences. Just know that whether there is so-called acceptance or so-called rejection it is all part of the flow you are in. It's a misconception to think, "I should be going with the flow more." You cannot *not* go with the flow, because you have no say in it at all. You are swept up in it despite yourself.

Once the yearning to know Self becomes intense and one-pointed, it does all the work. It consumes all other yearnings.

Desires of ownership and self-improvement are all based on hope and despair. Desiring to see beyond control is the fire that dispels *all* other desires.

I am so lost.
If you are beginning to feel lost, it probably means that the understandings you came with are losing some of their thunder.

But I just want to get rid of the "me" and that feels so impossible.
Why would you need to get rid of something that doesn't even exist? This "me" you are identified with is like a hypnotic suggestion. You didn't begin life with this "me" identity. The identities came afterwards, which means they are not innate, not natural to You. These identities come and go and are honed to suit certain circumstances. Then they are discarded. Today you think, "I am such a great person." Tomorrow you think, "I'm useless!" What has changed?

My attitudes.
And how is the experiencing of these attitudes possible?

Because I am!
And that sense of being never disappears—during waking and dreaming states—regardless of what experiences come your way. So why give focus to illusive identities that come and go all the time? They only bring you misery and increase the need to control. Your mind wasn't full of any needs when you first experienced being.

That experience of being hasn't stopped. It just *seems* to have changed because now you experience being some-body. Look to that which preceded these changes and continues to be there throughout all of them. Get to know this being-ness and figure out what it was prior to all the labels. All the answers lie there—at the point where the mind was free of concepts that misinterpreted You.

As a newborn infant spontaneity was the experience, though you didn't even have a word for it. Spontaneity is natural to you. Efforting started the minute you were taught that spontaneity isn't appropriate. That is when all the struggling began. It had a beginning you were aware of, which means it is a superimposition upon that which is innate and natural to You.

Spontaneity was the natural state when this being-ness began, although you probably only have a vague memory of that beginning. Effort and control are concepts that came unnaturally to you and still feel unnatural, or at least uncomfortable. They cause you anguish and deplete energy.

But the habits are so ingrained.
Despite these ingrained habits, you have daily glimpses of your spontaneous, essential nature. Every time you lose yourself in an activity, retrospectively you experience peace, efficiency of action, and freedom from efforting. Those glimpses are your greatest signpost. They point to what is natural—what "comes naturally." If you want to do something, play! Engage in activities in which you know you can easily lose yourself. Whether those are driving, playing golf, working on the computer. Do what comes naturally, and what comes unnaturally will gradually become less and less important to you.

And it isn't a matter of waiting until the weekend comes and you don't have to work. Stop focusing on this and that experience and recognize that experiences change all the time. The experiencing of them doesn't. Experiencing is always happening, and no particular experience changes this fact. If you understand this deeply, your focus will begin to turn away from individual experiences. Gradually, a newness will be there in the experiencing of *any* event—even situations you previously thought of as laborious or uninteresting.

You don't have to "wait for enlightenment" before you can experience life more fully. That would be like waiting for a plane to arrive that you are already sitting in.

But I can't stop working. I understand what you are saying, that even work can be enjoyable when I'm not judging it. I still feel it would be easier if I had more time doing things I really enjoyed.
Of course you can't stop working, and why should you? Do you enjoy your work?

No.
Would you rather have a job as a pilot, or an astronaut, or something exotic like that?

Yes, sure.
But that isn't the experience. Right now you have a job, but because you compare it to other jobs that you'd prefer, you probably just cope your way through the day. So, for five or six hours a day you focus on five o'clock and the moment you can go home.

What if you were in the middle of your workday and knew with absolute certainty that this moment were your last. You are unable to stop working, and you can't change your circumstances. What then?

I'd feel pretty depressed.
Ah, would you? Or would you experience that last moment as fully as possible? After all, you don't need to control it. It's going to be over in the next moment. All you have is that final moment.

117

I guess I would be totally present to it. But then again I might just sit there in fear.

And you'd be totally present to the fear then, wouldn't you, if it was all-consuming?

You see, you are never able to be absent from the moment. While you experience being, it means you experience being present, not absent or somewhere else. Even if thoughts are turned towards the past or the future, you can only experience them here and now.

Now tell me, how much of the time does the experience of being present contain boredom and thoughts about what might be and what will be?

Much of the time.

Then you are totally bored, and what is the benefit of that? And what is boredom but a state of comparing one situation to another. Boredom is nothing but a sign that you want to be absent from your experience as it *seems*. You want to be absent from what is as it is because it seems objectionable or boring.

You can only have the experience of boredom because you experience being present. You have no idea how the experience of being is possible, even though you attribute it to the body. Even though you think you know how and why you *are*, that is all just learned information.

How you experience being and why it *happened* is the greatest mystery. Yet you ignore the mystery, take it for granted, and focus on boredom. You focus on what *seems* to be, reject it, and don't for a moment wonder how the experiencing of it is possible.

The minute you begin deeply questioning this mystery, boredom is a thing of the past. Every instant provides you with the opportunity of fathoming this riddle. When you realize this, gradually what is being experienced loses importance. One activity is no more or less important than any other, because they all happen in relation to this consciousness you are trying to understand.

All experiences happen as a result of this "I amness," another word for which would be *experiencing*. When you realize that, and start trying to understand where this seed of consciousness sprouted from, you stop caring about results. All your focus turns towards trying to understand the principle that makes these experiences possible and away from the experiences themselves.

There is nothing complicated about this. The mind is programmed with divergent thoughts and is always distracting you with *this then that*. The mind has accumulated a collection of rigid preferences—this versus that. And you think them all so important and vital to your existence.

All that has to happen is that you lose interest in experiences and focus on the experiencing principle, which right now you know in terms of "I am."

One of the most useful things my teacher Wendell ever said to me was, "Lose interest in experiences." It took me a long time to understand what he meant, but now I'm imparting these same words to you. IF you begin to "get" what I'm saying it will change the way in which you experience *everything*.

Mind, you have given
Colors
To That which is
Colorless.

Lay down your
Paintbrush!
Give up your obsession
With coloring Me!

Heart, weighed down
By images
Of That which is
Imageless.

Stir the colors of
Mind
And paint "me"
Yearning.

Mind, you'll soon empty of
Struggling,
And color Me
Effortless.

Abstraction in your
Own right,
You can never grasp this
Knowing.

Consciousness and the Mind

The sense that I exist is very strong. I can't imagine that ever ending, although death seems to mean that.
Sometimes I think, "Maybe there is just this and then nothing."
Most people like to think otherwise. This is why the concepts of heaven, hell, the afterlife, past lives, etc. have come about. People can't conceive of nothing. Their sense of existing is so strong that they can't conceive of it ever really ending. This is because they think of themselves as some-*thing*: a body, a mind, and a bunch of labels. The only way they can conceive of existing after "death" is if this object carries on too. That's why heaven is such a satisfying notion.
"You-the-bundle-of-objects" goes up to a paradise where another object, God, is finally met. Or "you-the-bundle-of-objects" goes down to hell, and you don't even want to think about that possibility.
This chair is an object that you can see, touch, and sit in. What was this chair before it existed?

It wasn't. There was no chair. It wasn't anything, or there wasn't anything.
What was required before this chair could exist?

Someone who thought about making it. The materials that were necessary for building it.
What was there before the *some-one thinking about making the chair*? What was there before the materials that make up the chair?

Consciousness?
Don't be philosophical or complicated. Just tell me what existed prior to the maker of the chair and the materials required for the chair's construction.

Nothing. Empty space.
Nothing. Empty space. There you have two concepts, eh? Now, what was there before these two concepts?

No concepts. Nothing.
And as soon as you say, "No concepts, nothing," what has happened? You have attributed concepts to the non-conceptual. The absence of concepts cannot be described by concepts, can it?

No.
Even if you say there is only absence, immediately the presence of a concept is there. You can't imagine total absence. This is why you can't imagine your own absence.
All you know is the experience of presence. Unfortunately, this presence has been misinterpreted as *being an object* or a bundle of objects. This leaves you in a quandary because you can't imagine being absent, but what you have learned about "death" seems to indicate the absence of "you."
And when you hear that You aren't an object, you can only come to the conclusion that you are *nothing.*
Because this is inconceivable to you, one of the most convenient solutions is the belief that you are a soul or a spirit. You don't know what they are exactly but they sound good, and no-one has proven they don't exist. It's a comfortable belief that a lot of people enjoy because it doesn't require them to think any further. That's the whole problem. People don't want to think beyond their comfort zone.
The trouble is that *comfort zone* is full of struggle—so not comfortable at all. But perhaps it's a case of better-the-discomfort-you-know than risk searching beyond it and perhaps finding more discomfort. Perhaps the worst thing that could

happen is that you don't find any answers or solutions.

Perhaps. And as you say, it only happens in rare cases anyway, that the Self is realized.
When we use the word *realize,* it is usually in the context of someone realizing something. That means that someone has to be separate to something before it can be realized.
As you *are* the Self, how can you *realize* It? I know philosophical language talks of Self-realization, but that's just a term. It's a confusing one too. You see, who You really are already Is. Your experience of that Is-ness is registered by the mind in the words "I am." Another word for this Is-ness is Consciousness. You are conscious of being, but to that sense of presence you have added labels. "I am conscious of being intelligent." "I am conscious of being skinny." "I am conscious of being angry." All the appearances—the labels—change constantly. What doesn't change?

The consciousness of being doesn't change.
Yes. And if you are trying to find out what the essential nature of something is, you have to discover what is unchanging about it.
If clay is made into a bird, then a cow, then a vase, what would you tell a blind person you are looking at—an ever-changing object?

No. I'd tell them it was clay being molded into different objects.
Yes. To explain what something is, you have to look at what is unchanging about it. So, if you want to know Your essential nature, it stands to reason you have to look at what is unchanging about you, doesn't it? And that is.....?

Consciousness.
During waking and dreaming states you are conscious of yourself. So Consciousness is the closest you can come to a constant while you are identified with the body.
Now let's look at this word *Consciousness* because it has many interpretations and connotations. On the one hand, it means "to

123

be aware of one's surroundings and identity." This form of consciousness describes "I-amness." But when the body is deemed "dead" this consciousness ends. What do you think is left?

Nothing. The absence of consciousness.
Let's say you are the sky—a conscious sky—with a cloud appearing in you. Will the appearance of this cloud affect you in any way?

I'd be a cloudy sky. (laughing)
But would you-the-sky really be permanently altered in any way? Would you be altered at all? Would you no longer be the sky?

No. I'd still be the sky.
What would have changed is that a cloud has appeared in you. But a cloud doesn't touch the sky, doesn't smudge it, doesn't take the place of the sky, or leave a hole in it when it's gone. As the sky, you remain unaffected, unaltered by anything that appears in you.
Now let's say that as the sky you have nothing to compare yourself to. There is just you-the-sky. Suddenly a cloud appears in you, and you experience yourself in relation to some-thing else. What happens?

Well, as the sky, I am. I just am. When the cloud appears, I know that there is something other than me.
Does this appearance of the "other" make you any more or less than you are?

No. I have something to compare myself to. I experience something other than myself.
Ah, but would you have been able to experience yourself without something to compare yourself to?

I don't know.

You don't know. But say you had always been just the sky; you'd never seen anything, you just were. This is all hypothetical, of course, but do you think there would have been thoughts about anything, or thoughts about yourself?

Well, I guess not.
Why do you guess not?

I wouldn't have thought about any "things" that's for sure, not if I'd never seen any.
But you think you might have thought about yourself?

I guess I'd just have been a very bored sky then. (laughing)
Think about it. If you are infinite, undifferentiated, with nothing to compare yourself to, would there be thoughts about yourself? Would there be thoughts of boredom? Would there be any fears, guilt, or desires?

I suppose boredom and desires only happen in relation to things. If I'm not a thing and don't know any other things, I suppose I wouldn't even be bored with myself. Ah, no; so I wouldn't have had thoughts about myself!
Are you saying then that there would be no thoughts at all?

Yes. What would I think about? No, there wouldn't be any thoughts. I'd just be.
But you wouldn't know it would you?
You tell me. How do you know anything?

Because I am.
Yes, but how do you know that?

The mind knows it. The mind has thoughts about it. It thinks "I am."
The mind doesn't think. It *is* thoughts. *Thinking* describes the experiencing of those thoughts.
Now, let's stick with this hypothetical sky for a moment. The appearance of the cloud gives you-the-sky a sense of self in

125

relation to something else. But when the cloud disappears, do you also disappear?

No. I continue being the sky.
Now let's go back to You. The body appears with other objects and this is reflected in the mind as thoughts. These thoughts link You to objects, and You then identify with these objects and the belief arises, that "I am some-body," "I am this and that." This is like the sky registering the appearance of a cloud and thinking, "I am cloudy."

So what is the mind?
The mind is the language of Consciousness, or the interpretation of it in thoughts. Oftentimes, the mind is referred to as "the light of Consciousness."
I remember when I first heard this term that I struggled with it. This was probably because, at that time, my mind still felt like one big clutter of confused thoughts. It was hard to understand it in terms of having anything to do with light.
It helped once I understood that light is actually imperceptible. You only ever see objects that are illuminated by it. You never see light as such.
Once I understood this it became clear that, if objects are only apparent because of light, the source of light can't be an object. This is when I started to grasp that the mind doesn't have any real or autonomous "existence". It is just a phenomenal reflector or reflection of the light of Consciousness.
Until then, because I was strongly identified with the mind, I still thought in terms of the mind *causing* thoughts. That is, I still thought that Consciousness was something that was made possible by the mind. I didn't understand that it was the other way round.
The mind isn't the cause of Self-consciousness. It is merely the mechanism that picks up the light of Consciousness.
Once I understood this it was just a matter of simple deduction. The mind reflects the light of Consciousness in the knowing "I am." Prior to the appearance of the mind the light of

Consciousness had to be at rest in its source, which could not it-Self BE light.

This told me that the mind, like any reflector, was giving me a reverse image of my True, non-dual nature.

This reaffirmed what I had understood, but was still grappling with; that the mind cannot know who or what I really am. It can only give me an indication of who I am NOT.

But when we are first born the mind doesn't do this does it? I mean, there aren't any thoughts about self.

In the newborn infant the mind is rather like a clear piece of glass that catches the light of Consciousness, but doesn't distort or refract it. There is simply the wordless knowing "I am", or the wordless sense of presence.

With the onset of interaction with the world the mind becomes not only the reflector of the light of Consciousness, but also the reflector of everything in manifestation that is illuminated by this *light*.

When this starts happening the mind is better likened to a prism in that the combination of "I am-consciousness" plus other objects is refracted in the thought form "I am this and that."

Just because a prism refracts light and gives it the appearance of colors, it hasn't changed the essential nature of light in any way. Similarly, just because the mind refracts or breaks up the light of Consciousness into the thought "I am this and that," the essential nature of Consciousness remains unchanged.

We could say that Your original nature is Consciousness at rest. This would mean that Your original nature is both void of light and color. Spontaneously Consciousness "stirs" and we can call this "stirring" the *light* of Consciousness. This results in the appearance of manifestation. This means that You the Absolute are Self-illuminating or Self-effulgent.

While the mind is oriented towards manifestation Consciousness is misinterpreted to be caused by an object, and you think that You *are* this object.

If you learn that this is a misperception, and if this understanding is intuited to hold some truth, the mind starts orienting away from you-the-person.

As the mind orients towards the light of Consciousness or Self the mind boots us less and less dogmatic information about the pseudo-you.

In this way, the "this and that" that has been added to "I am" is gradually seen in a clearer perspective. If this process continues, Self-consciousness goes from being an awkward, distorted interpretation or reflection of Self to being a clear knowing. You know who You are not.

However, this "knowing" is expressed via your unique intellect or "I." This means that light of Consciousness is still being refracted. The difference is that you have a clearer perspective on these refractions. This gradual shift in perspective describes the process of enlightenment.

In rare cases, when the mind orients fully away from the "I," all the thought-refractions about Self cease.

If you look through a hollow tube, the diameter of which directly encompases the sun, you are blinded by the light and cannot see its source.

Similarly, when the mind orients fully towards the light of Consciousness, thought processes are "cancelled out."

The objects of manifestation continue being illuminated by the light of Consciousness, but this *light* is no longer deviated or refracted via a particular mind. This is when You the non-dual Subject have direct, objective Knowledge of Self in relation to *duality*.

This is very different to knowing about Your Self via a particular aspect of duality.

Relatively speaking, the embodiment of this Knowledge is often called Sat-guru.

What happens when we are in deep sleep, or un-conscious?
In deep sleep Consciousness is at rest. That is, the light of Consciousness ceases illuminating the mind and you are unaware of yourself. There is simply Awareness, unaware of It-Self. This is why deep sleep is the most natural state. It is Your Original state.

As Nisargadatta used to say, (and I paraphrase) "this is why the 'twilight zone' between deep sleep and waking holds the most clues to You."

You make it sound like the waking state is a pathology!
In deep sleep, there is total peace. Why is that?

I don't know that I am and so don't have anything to worry about. (laughing)
Total peace happens when you are unaware of the pseudo-you. You are at-ease. Then, as soon as you and other objects appear, the peace becomes some degree or other of dis-ease. Another word for this so-called dis-ease state is awkward self-consciousness or *ignorance*. You are ignorant of Your Self.
If you have to focus on one thing, your focus is turned away from other things. If you didn't know this chair was in the room and just saw the table, you would be ignorant of the chair.
Phenomenality is the contrasting of one object against another. This contrasting of objects is refracted or broken up into various thought-images in the mind.
The facets of a prism catch the light, which shines through the piece of glass. Because the surface of the prism is uneven, the light meets obstacles. The light is contrasted against these *obstacles* and the resulting contrast gives the appearance of colors.
The word *mind* describes a collection of thoughts. Let's say these thoughts are the *colors* of the mind. Can you experience the absence of thoughts?

Well, retrospectively. When I meditate, the mind stills and there are no thoughts. I guess I only know that in retrospect.
If you know something retrospectively, does that mean you have a direct experience of it?

No. I have a memory now of something that happened in the past.
While no thoughts are present, there is total ignorance about their absence. When "I am-consciousness" is absent in deep sleep, or as a newborn infant, is awareness absent?

There's awareness, but I'm not aware of it. I'm not conscious of it.

You are ignorant of awareness, but that doesn't mean awareness is absent, does it? When you wake up, retropsectively, you know this is the case.

In light of this understanding, one could say the mind IS ignorance. The mind is the holder of the "I am" thought, which comes and then disappears in deep sleep or when you say, "For a moment there I forgot myself."

In those waking hours when you "forget yourself," Your essential nature expresses it-Self uninhibitedly. When you focus on yourself in relation to "others," spontaneity is lost. Then Your essential, spontaneous nature takes on the appearance of struggling.

Can you explain the word phenomenon? I kind of know what it means but....

A *phenomenon* is an inexplicable appearance. The mind is a phenomenon—an inexplicable appearance, amid other inexplicable appearances.

One can say that there is only Awareness—but Awareness is just another concept, another description. It's not a solution, do understand that.

In Awareness unaware of it-Self, spontaneously there arises the appearance of *mind* in relation to objects. This is a phenomenon, an inexplicable appearance.

The mind isn't any "thing" you can touch, but you have perception of it. How do you have a perception of the mind? How is it possible that you know about the mind?

Because I have one!

Ah, this is how you answer while you believe You *are* the mind. It's only because you think you *are* the mind that you are so confused. The mind is no different to a mirror, in that it enables You to see Your reflection in the information "I am." It's because of the mind that you know about yourself, but the mind has no experience of you. It is simply a data bank, and like any data bank it can't see or experience the information it holds.

The mind holds the information "I am," along with misinterpretations of that information.

Could the mind *be* without awareness?

No.

We are limited by language, but that's our medium, so we'll call Your True nature no-thingness for now.

The mind dis-appears, and re-appears *in* no-thingness. This means that the mind, and that which it reflects—"I amness," the body, and other objects—are *all* made of the same *stuff*—no-thingness.

Clearly, something cannot be created out of nothing. This means that "things" do not exist.

Inexplicably the mind reflects the contrast of "I am" and the body, and you experience existing. The mind then links the "I am" and the body together and the misinterpretation, "I am some-body," is booted up.

This misinterpretation is then attributed to other bodies and unique expressions of consciousness. You think you are an object and so is every-one else. This gives rise to the experience of separateness.

But if you try and contrast the "I amness" that's happening via your body, and the "I amness" happening through my body, what happens?

Well, my personality is different from yours.
Yes, your personality is different from mine. But can you compare your experience of being to mine?

I experience being confused. You probably experience being peaceful all the time. (laughing)
I have all kinds of experiences, the same way you do. Intellectually you break experiencing up into this and that experience. Various experiences are only possible because there

is the experience of being. As long as there is a body, there will be endless experiences.

That which is experiencing via your body is of the same *stuff* as That which is experiencing via my body. It doesn't matter through which body Consciousness is expressing it-Self. It's all still Consciousness, or Experiencing. But because you think of yourself as an object you believe experiences can affect "you." I know I am not any object, and that I am the impersonal functioning or experiencing of Totality. So experiences don't affect Me in any way. There is still experiencing happening and there are still various experiences. The difference is I know that "I" remain unaffected and unchanged by any experience.

Does your experience, your knowledge that you exist, differ from my knowledge that I exist?

Well, you know you aren't a body. I still experience myself as being the body, although I understand otherwise.

Forget the differences in experience and knowledge. I'm not talking about any other experience than the knowledge "I exist." After all, I don't think I exist any more or less than you. I just know there is much, much less of Me than you think there is of you. (laughing)

Okay. There isn't any difference. I get that.

There are *relative* experiential differences, but Consciousness expressing It-Self through my body is exactly the same as Consciousness expressing It-Self through your body.

Right now you are focused on apparent differences, but those *apparent* differences aren't anything real. They appear and disappear.

When your body is in deep sleep, and mine is in deep sleep, what is the difference in awareness happening through the two bodies?

There isn't any.

In deep sleep Awareness is unaware of It-Self, but it's still there. Then you wake up and you know "I am"; and Awareness is still there—now conscious of It-Self. This means that Awareness unaware of It-Self, and Self-consciousness, are one and the same. You the Absolute and manifest-You are not-two. This is the meaning of Advaita, the philosophy of non-dualism. *Advaita* means *not-two*.

How do we get to see beyond the distorted image of self?
It's not a matter of seeing *beyond* the distorted image. It's really a matter of being absolutely clear that what you are seeing isn't You; that it's a distortion, an aberration.
Like a mirror, the mind only offers you a reflection of Self. And a reflection is never the real thing, is it? Also, a reflection is always a reverse image of what is being reflected. The reverse image of You the non-dual Absolute, unaware of Your Self, is self-consciousness in relation to "others" or duality.
Let's say you go into one of those mirror arcades. In each mirror you see a different image of yourself. In one, your body is short and fat. In the other, it's long and thin. Then you go home and stand in front of your own mirror and see a non-distorted reflection of your body. Has your body changed in any way because of any of the mirrors it was reflected in?

No.
You have total conviction that your body is not any of the distorted reflections you saw. You don't need to see beyond the reflections to know that the body is not distorted. All you need to do is be convinced that your body is NOT the reflection.
It's the same when it comes to knowing your essential nature or Self. You just have to realize, beyond a shadow of a doubt, that you are not what you *think*.

Okay! That helped a lot.
Then you know who you Really are, at last! (laughing)
What do you mean "at last"? The knowing "I am" is already there. You know about this "I amness" already. All that has happened is that superimposed upon the knowing "I am," is the idea "I am this and that." If you realize that the "this and that" isn't You, have You changed in any way?

133

No.
So it isn't a matter of "Knowing who You really are at last." It is just that "knowing" is no longer attributed to an object.
Knowing or *experiencing* is Your essential, manifest nature. Once you realize You are not an object "having" experiences it doesn't mean you know who or what You really are. It means you know who You are not.
You can never Know who or what, You really Are, because You are beyond explanation, and beyond the *need* to know anything. You already are and this whole world illusion is nothing but an appearance You the non-apparent Absolute have assumed.
In the assuming of this appearance, experiencing began. At first experiencing was attributed to the bodymind. Now you are beginning to understand otherwise and you call experiencing "seeking."
All you need to understand is that You are the source of *seeking*, the source of *experiencing*. The trouble is that the mind boots up the misinformation that "it" is doing the seeking.

So the mind knows I am, but doesn't really know it? Is that what you're saying.
The mind doesn't "know" anything. The mind is the holder of information about manifestation. It reflects this information in thoughts, but it has no experience of them. The mind IS information. The mind isn't experiencing thoughts.
The mind is just like a computer that boots information up on its screen. The computer screen has no knowledge of the words. It is merely the holder, or reflector of them.
The problem arises when you start thinking, "I am the mind," which is what you infer when you say "I am intelligent," "I am silly." When you learn You aren't the mind, your identity or sense of self is threatened. The mind reflects this new data in confused thoughts.

And the ego? What is that?

134

The ego describes the sense of presence, the sense of self. So to talk about "getting rid of the ego," as many people do, is an impossible, crazy notion.

One could say that the distorted sense of presence is the unhealthy ego. But the ego isn't something that you need to get rid of. It just needs to first be strong—that is when self-esteem is healthier, even if it is because you think everything happens *because* of you. Then, when it is strong enough, you are ready to learn that everything happens *despite* you. So the ego isn't something to "get rid of."

But then the mind and the ego sound as if they are one and the same thing?

The mind reflects the sense of presence in the thought "I am." It puts words to the sense of presence. Your essential nature IS the knowing "I Am." When the body is deemed "dead," it's because this knowing is no longer animating it. Who you Really are is beyond knowing and not-knowing. Your True nature is That which preceded the knowing of self and is That which now *has* Knowledge of it. While this knowledge is filtered via the mind you know about Your Self indirectly.

I'm getting a clearer understanding, but it's still very superficial. I know I'm not the body or the mind, I understand that. But I still don't experience not being them!

And that's all that has to happen; that gradually, or suddenly, the false self is recognized for what it is – NOT You. As the understanding goes deeper, gradually the experience of "you" will change.

I hope so!

That doesn't mean you will stop experiencing being. That's what you need to understand. It's just that you will stop experiencing being some-thing. You'll still experience this in relation to the bodymind. That is the paradox of it, that you'll know you are not a bodymind, but because this knowing happens via the bodymind you will still be identified *with* it.

135

The difference is you will no longer be identified *as* it.
This is the first step; that orientation shifts away from *you* in
terms of "being" an object.
This shift in orientation will be reflected in the mind in thoughts
that are less and less involved. Thoughts will still come and go,
but you-the-person will finally fall into perspective.

Don't you mean that me-the-person won't exist anymore?
No. You-the-person has never existed. You-the-person is nothing
more than a mirage, an image that has been superimposed
upon the Absolute, which is imageless.
If your reflection appears in a mirror and when you walk away
the mirror hasn't changed in any way. The reflection never
touched the mirror. Temporarily, it just changed its appearance.
A change in appearance doesn't constitute any real change. It's
a relative change, but the word *relative* signifies non-absolute.
If something is non-absolute and impermanent you can't say it
has any real, autonomous existence.

I don't get it.
Something cannot be created out of nothing. The word *exist*
denotes an undoubted presence. If *something* comes and goes
within *no-thingness,* does that mean that both something and
no-thingness both *exist*?

The "something" exists temporarily.
The word *exist* indicates an undoubted presence. If something is
here today and gone tomorrow, when it's gone can you be sure
that it was ever there?

*I guess it could just have been my imagination, so no, I can't be
sure it was ever there.*
Another word for the mind could be *imagination*. The mind
reflects images. These images come and go, so you can't say
they really exist. These images only "exist" *in relation to* other
images. If something "exists" in relation to something else, that
describes *relativity*. Relativity is not reality.

And that's why you are in this mess of believing you are something You are not. You have mistaken relativity for Reality.

But how can I tell what is real and what is unreal? I keep on trying really hard to see what is unreal.
If you can see something, it's not real. So your problem is solved! (laughing)
Appearances come and go, so they have no *absolute* existence. Who You really are is Absolute and eternal, and that describes Existence in the true sense. Existence doesn't describe anything fleeting or impermanent. All that can happen is that this understanding goes deeper and deeper. It's not a matter of seeing *beyond* appearances. It's just a matter of having a clearer and clearer perspective on them. Then gradually, or fast, *Self in relation to appearances* will fall into perspective. You'll realize you are not them and that's the first stage, realizing who you are NOT.

When experiences change has the act of experiencing *changed in any way?*
Surely the question is not "How do I control experiences?" but "How is the experiencing of anything possible?"

As a "seeker" you are conscious of the idea "I do not know My Self."
The question is, who or what is conscious of this idea?

Thoughts and Thinking

*I'm finding it really difficult to "get" that thoughts and thinking are different. You say, "The mind **is** thoughts," but we do say, "The mind thinks."*

Intuitively, you know that thoughts and thinking are different. This is clear when you say, "I am thinking certain thoughts," or "I'm having certain thoughts."

The reason I emphasize the difference between thoughts and thinking is because you are strongly identified with thoughts. You feel pride, guilt, and frustration in relation to thoughts because you believe they represent you.

The watching or experiencing of thoughts is what is called *thinking*. That you use such terms as, "I'm watching the thoughts that come up in my mind," tells you that you are separate from those thoughts. You can't watch or experience anything unless you are separate to it. Simple logic tells you that you cannot BE something you can watch or experience. You have to be separate from it.

So where do emotions come in? I mean, different thoughts bring up different emotions.

Throughout the day, when you are awake, you experience thoughts. Although many of them may not elicit strong feelings, there's a constant subtle—and sometimes not so subtle—shifting in the way you feel. This means that thoughts and feelings are inextricably interlinked.

I'm not so well versed on psychoanalytical language. Perhaps there is a specific way of explaining the difference between feelings and emotions. I just see emotions—joy, fear, sadness, grief, anger, and worry—as being the labels that distinguish this feeling from that feeling. In the end, it's all just *experiencing*.

139

Your essential nature is impersonal, spontaneous experiencing. In other words, Your manifest appearance *is* experiencing. Manifest-Self IS *experiencing*. One aspect of Experiencing is *thinking*. Another aspect of experiencing is *feeling* or having emotions. Even if you break experiencing up into explanations such as fearing, grieving, enjoying, and struggling, its still *experiencing*.

Because you think you are an object, you believe that whatever happens in relation to "you" can affect and change you. You experience an event and thoughts about it give rise to various emotions. Then you identify with both thoughts—the mind—and your emotional reaction to them. When you say, "I am so angry," this is literally what you believe—that you *are* the emotion of anger. As there are so many emotions you don't like (such as fear, anger, grief, sadness), you have a vested interest in suppressing or avoiding these emotions. When you can't suppress certain emotions you feel bad about yourself. This is because you are not only identified with emotions, but also believe that you should be able to control them. That's about as ridiculous as believing a dog's tail has control over the dog. (laughing)

While people identify with emotions and thoughts it's not surprising that they feel they have to do affirmations all day long and go to self-love seminars, or take drugs to suppress these emotions. It's rather like being a demented Neptune trying to hold the ocean at bay. Because emotions are always in flux, you feel out of control most of the time.

So the mind—can you talk a little more on the mind?

No-one has ever found the mind, and for the longest time the brain was considered the physical organ that generated thoughts. But the brain is nothing more than a lump of tissue animated by Consciousness. The brain itself is not the generator of thoughts. It's just an inanimate object animated by Consciousness, as is every aspect of the body.

More recently it has been discovered that neuro-peptides, or brain tissue, are not solely isolated to the brain. It's found in the connective tissue throughout the body. So there is actually more brain tissue outside the brain than in it. And there's a particularly large concentration of neuro-peptides found in the connective tissue behind the stomach. This is an interesting discovery because the stomach and solar plexus area could be said to be the seat of the distorted (perception of) ego.

The word *ego* describes the sense of presence, or the sense of being that you experience. While the sense "I am" is being misinterpreted as "I am some-body," the sense of presence is experienced primarily in the solar plexus area. Once you deeply realize that you aren't "some-body," your distorted sense of self begins losing its distortions. Then the sense of presence is predominately felt in the Heart center. This is why the Heart is considered the seat of Self.

The Self, or Consciousness, has no location and is not isolated to or limited by the body. This isn't your experience, however, as long as you believe you are "some-body." While this belief predominates, you think that "you"—this lump of flesh and bones—are subject to limitation, and you believe that certain emotions are best avoided because they appear to affect "you" in a way you don't like.

When breath cycles are full, they cause the diaphragm to rise up and down which massages the underlying organs. As each organ has concordances to various emotions, the synthesizing of emotions can only happen when full breath cycles occur.

I remember when emotional "holdings" or "storings" began releasing in my body. I noticed a dramatic change in my breathing patterns. At first I was so unused to breathing fully and deeply that I was almost surprised not to feel a draft on my feet. This is when I began to notice a tremendous change in the solar plexus area. Although I had been unaware of it until then, the solar plexus had always felt extremely dense. Once the "holdings" dissolved I experienced, and continue to experience, an unbelievable lightness in that area of the body. Actually the whole body feels that way, whereas, prior to this dissolution, the solar plexus tension just used to radiate out. The whole body would easily tense when emotions arose.

Before I go on, do remember that the ego doesn't have a location. The word simply describes the sense of presence or experience of being that is felt in relation to the body. I'm just giving you imagery, so do keep that in perspective.

That what we'll call the "unhealthy" ego is *located* in the solar plexus area makes sense because most of the major organs are situated near and around that area—lungs, liver, spleen, stomach, kidneys, heart—and they all have concordances to emotions, which are rarely experienced fully while you think you are the bodymind.

What are those concordances?

The lungs are associated with the emotion grief. The liver has a concordance with the emotion of anger. The stomach and spleen relate to worry. The kidneys relate to the emotion of fear. The lungs relate to grief and the heart to joy and sadness.

Rigid beliefs trigger, or are accompanied by, various degrees of grief, fear, worry, and anger. So it stands to reason that when dogmatic thoughts give way to uncensored ones, the solar plexus is going to "lighten up." (laughing)

While you are identified with dogmatic beliefs and self-esteem is particularly low, the solar plexus can feel very weak. If self-esteem is high, the solar plexus can feel like a powerhouse. Either way, as long as the sense of presence is linked to an object-identity, the solar plexus is experienced as very dense. So much energy goes into maintaining emotional "holdings," particularly in the solar plexus. This is why, while you identify with emotions, the Heart center, or seat of Self, can never be fully experienced.

But we feel the emotion of love in the heart?

Love is not an emotion. Love is the mental interpretation of the lack of involvement. When no dogmatic beliefs arise vis-a-vis the object of your affection, you don't put up any "fronts." Various emotions may arise, but as long as they are unaccompanied by thoughts of "Why" and "Will it last?", these emotions are felt fully.

To experience emotions fully is rare, because the habit is to censor them. You want to feel more joy, less anger, etc. In the rare instances you experience emotions fully you experience peace.

Censorship is absent and this feels liberating and peaceful. What human beings refer to as *love*, is simply the absence of censorship which translates into peace or neutrality.

It is a total misconception that experiences can give or take away your sense of peace. No experience can affect You because Your True nature *is* absolute Peace—although Peace is just a word and not a description of You. It is your attitude towards experiences that's the only "problem." The need to censor and cling onto different experiences is what disrupts your sense of peace. Experiences themselves have never ever been a problem. Your misinterpretation of them has come about because of your misinterpretation of self as an object, which is the victim of experiences.

But we feel peace or love in the heart.

Yes, you usually do. The mind is considered one of the "coverings" of the Heart. When there are no rigid opinions in the mind, the Heart center is felt. Temporarily, the false facades come down and you feel you can just "be yourself." That is when you get a glimpse of what is most natural to you—spontaneity and the lack of prejudice. You call this neutrality *peace* or *love*.

So what is memory? Sorry, I'm still trying to figure out the mind.

Questions are good. (laughing)

As one of the functions of the mind is memory, most people still think that memory is located in the head. However, nowadays it has been discovered that memories are actually stored in all aspects of the body—the blood, the bones, the cells, the muscles etc.

This became particularly clear to me once I trained as a bodyworker. Frequently, when a muscle would release in the body of a patient I was working with, they would recall traumatic or happy memories. These memories were triggered, and to some degree or other synthesized when the muscular "holding" gave way. After a while I began to think of the body rather like a robot covered in detonation buttons.

I'm afraid I'm being slow, but I'm still struggling with the difference between thoughts and thinking.

143

You believe thoughts are personal. This is why you say, "These are *my* thoughts." But just because certain thoughts are unique to your particular bodymind doesn't make them personal or "yours." The thoughts you experience are unique to you, but they aren't personal and you don't own them or have any control over them. The fact that you think you own thoughts means you intuit that you are separate to them. After all, you can't own something and BE it. It's the same with the body. You say "my body," so clearly you can't BE the body because you talk in terms of ownership.

Apparently experiments have been done which show that the witnessing of any event registers up to half a second later in the brain. This includes actions that you believe you have affected with personal volition. For example, the thought comes to raise an arm and the raising of the arm happens. The experience is that the thought precedes the action you decide upon. Science has now shown that the action actually happens first, and the mind only knows about it a split second later. This is pretty good evidence that actions happen despite you, eh?

But you don't need to rely on scientific "proofs." After all, science is fallible.

You're better relying on your own "personal" investigation of this. (laughing) Just sit there and raise your arm and tell me how you did it?

I don't know.

And even science doesn't know how actions come about. You think actions are personal and happen because you decide on them. Yet you have don't have the faintest idea how movement is possible. You think you make decisions, but you don't have the foggiest idea how thoughts come about or how thinking happens. Although you are ignorant of how functioning is possible, you take credit for it and experience pride or guilt for whatever actions happen. Ridiculous, eh! (laughing)

But isn't volition the ability to act? If actions are registered in the brain up to half a second after they happen, then thinking— which is an action—must also happen up to half a second after a thought happens.

144

Good, now you're beginning to differentiate between thoughts and thinking, eh? (laughing) You are partially right, but the word *volition* means "desire or choice." The word *volition* means the desire to act. It doesn't mean the ability to act.

Thinking is the word we use to describe *the experiencing of thoughts*. To say, "I'm thinking a thought" describes a subject-object relationship. That you experience thinking thoughts tells you that *thoughts,* and *the act of thinking* are inextricably interlinked yet different.

According to the findings of that scientific experiment, events and actions only register in the brain up to half a second before they actually happen. One could say that the arising of a desirous thought is an *event* and that thinking is an *action*. If you understand this deeply enough, you'll realize that no desires are personal and no thoughts or actions are personal. This means that you are not responsible for anything that happens. Everything happens despite you, and you only know about it up to half a second after it has happened.

To understand this is to realize that guilt is just a fanciful notion and that it has absolutely no validity. Now put the understandings, "Everything happens despite me," and "Guilt is invalid" together. Here you have two pretty good indications that what you believe about yourself is desperately in need of re-evaluation, eh? (laughing)

I reckon!

Maybe this is a really silly question, but is there a difference between knowledge and knowing? I mean, you make a difference between thoughts and thinking.
It's not a silly question. Yes, there is a relative difference between knowledge and knowing.

Your essential nature or manifest appearance *is knowing*. By *knowing,* I refer to the sense of being, or the experience "I am." In the process of learning that you are a limited object subject to *shoulds* and *should nots*, this "knowing" has taken on a distorted appearance.

145

A word we sometimes use to describe knowing is *intuiting*, which means immediate or direct insight. Learned information has distorted this direct insight into Your essential nature. The good news is that even though your perception of Self is faulty, Your essential nature isn't hidden from you.

When you say, "I find it so easy to be myself with so and so," it's because with that person you stop judging yourself and your actions. The knowing or intuiting is there that when judgments and censorship of actions is absent, you experience being Your Self.

These two terms, "being myself" and "not being myself," are ones everyone uses. Strangely, few people recognize that the use of these terms signify that everyone, however rigid their programming, has direct insight into their essential nature. The knowing is always there as to who you are NOT. You just miss all the clues that your language holds.

Intuitively you also know that thoughts and thinking are different. If this weren't the case, why would you say, "I am thinking certain thoughts," or "I'm having certain thoughts"?

The knowing is also there that you are not the body or the mind. If this weren't the case, why would you say, "I am *in* the body" and "I *have* a mind"? These expressions show that you intuit you are not the body or the mind and that you are separate to them. After all, you can't be located in relation to something and BE it, and you can't own something and BE it.

As a so-called seeker, you think you are looking for something that's hidden from you. Your essential nature is never hidden. It's just that your perception of it is faulty. Self isn't hidden; it's just that you have bought into certain programming that causes you to perceive Self incorrectly.

Enlightenment describes the absolute conviction that You are not the bodymind or any other object. *Conviction* in this context has nothing to do with the mind. What is meant is that *learned* descriptions of self give way to knowing that is beyond words and descriptions.

You see, Your essential nature is never absent or hidden from you. It is just that knowing has been veiled in pseudo-logic and learned information, which gives you a faulty perception of Self.

As a result, you *appear* to be other than You are.

What do you mean?
You have learned that you are the cause of what you experience. This changes your experience of actions—they feel like a personal effort and you feel guilt or pride because of them.

Actions have taken on the *appearance* of personal struggling and efforting, but this doesn't mean that any action is personal or *caused* by you. Despite your misperception of actions, they continue to happen as the result of impersonal functioning. This means that Your essential nature is never hidden from you. You just have a faulty perception of it.

Ah, okay. I just wish I really KNEW that as an experience! (laughing)
Have you never said, "I just want to be myself"?

Yes.
When you act in an inhibited way, the thought comes "I'm not being myself." This tells you that efforted actions are not natural to you. It also tells you that the "person" you *think* is causing these actions is NOT YOU. As those actions aren't being caused by "you," who is causing them?

I don't know.
When you use the word *cause* it means you are giving a *reason* to what is happening. You intuit that inhibited actions are nothing to do with YOU because when they happen you say, "I'm not being myself." You can't possibly BE somebody else when inhibited actions are happening. However, you are identified with actions, which means they define you.

When actions are inhibited and you experience not being yourself, are the actions happening from the standpoint of another body?

No.
But you believe you are the bodymind. If actions are happening

from the perspective of your bodymind, and IF you *are* it, how can you be being other than yourself, whatever actions are happening? If you think about this a little you'll realize that the belief "I am some-body," and the belief "I am what I do," contradict each other most of the time.

What you think you are looking for is glaring you in the face. You already know who you are NOT, but rigid conditioning prevents you from realizing this. (laughing) It's so simple!

You see, the knowing of who you are not is there and has never been hidden from you. You have just never paid attention to the language you use about yourself.

The knowing is there, and that *knowing* IS Your essential nature.

And knowledge...?

Knowledge means the sum-total of what is known and not-known. In what is called Self-realization, the knowing, "I am some-body" disappears. When this distortion to knowing subsides, it becomes quite clear that you are not any-body. However, there isn't direct Knowledge of this because, paradoxically, you still experience Self via an object.

During the waking states there is Self-knowing, and during deep sleep there is not-knowing about Your Self. This means that your knowing of Self is still indirect. This means that you don't have direct Knowledge of the sum total of what is known and not-known. You only have an indirect experience of it.

The jnani—or one who knows—no longer thinks of himself as the body, but he still experiences duality via this body and via the mind. The knowing is that these mechanisms are impersonal and have no bearing on Self. It is quite clear that You are not an object, but duality continues to be experienced from the perspective of an object. This means that you have an indirect experience of being the non-objective Subject.

When duality ceases being experienced from the perspective of a particular bodymind, there is direct Knowledge of the sum total of knowing or not-knowing, which is also termed *duality*. The indirect knowing that was happening in the unique bodymind of the jnani has subsided into direct Knowledge. Relatively speaking, this Knowledge is embodied in what is called Sat-guru.

148

Now that you know who you are... I mean, know that you know who you are not (laughing), what does it feel like?
Maybe I can give you a sense of this. You know how it is when you experience an extreme situation and you feel tension in the core of your being? That is never the experience any more. No experience feels all-permeating or as if it goes to the "core." Experiences seem to float on the surface as it were. It's rather like being a deep, still ocean with sometimes stormy and sometimes small waves happening on your surface.

You used to spend a lot of time in retreat. Do you still do that?
I'm so unconcerned by what is going on in the world around me now that I don't go out much. That's why I have these evenings only very rarely.
When I can, I prefer alone time, but this was always my nature. It just manifested to a lesser degree than now.
When I first began experiencing the body as what I can only call transparent, a certain amount of physical and mental adaptation was necessary. Until then, the "me" idea was like a suit of armor. Once the sense of armoring fell away, the experience of the body was suddenly very different. Then it just felt more nurturing sometimes to have alone time while adaptation to this happened.

My suit of armor just seems to feel heavier and heavier.
That you experience this "suit of armor" means you are aware of how unnatural your experience of yourself is. That's a beginning. Most people are oblivious to their armoring and think that how they feel is quite natural.
I'm not sure how best to explain it, but the old wave and ocean analogy comes to mind. Think of all the bodymind-identified expressions of Consciousness as being waves. Depending on how rigid their identities are, they will clash against each other and the waves will appear rougher. The jnani has stopped believing he is the bodymind so, minus rigid identities, he could be likened to a peaceful aspect of the surface of the ocean. This means that the

149

surrounding waves or bodymind-identified expressions of Con-sciousness have nothing to bump up against and so tend to easily subside in the presence of the jnani.

For a while, a year or so ago, my experience of this was is as if other expressions of Consciousness or personalities were being dissolved via my body. At first this was experienced as physically quite traumatic. That's when I found it easier to have periodic times of isolation.

But I thought you didn't experience "others"?
I know that there is no real "other," but unique expressions of consciousness happening through all the various bodyminds are still apparent to me. Whereas years ago I used to experience feeling other people and "their" unique energetic makeup, now there is absolutely no energetic sense of any "other."

But if you experienced dissolving their "holdings" in your body isn't that an energetic experience?
What I mean by an *energetic experience* of "others" is that while I was still ignorant of Self, I used to interpret what I called "other peoples' stuff" as feeling very different to "mine." I would feel a huge shift in energy when I was around certain people and could tell them to a tee what they were experiencing. Not that I did this, but their feedback usually confirmed what I was experiencing.

When I realized I wasn't any-body, for a while I experienced this phenomenon of dissolving "other peoples'" conditioning in my body. It had a whole different dynamic to it. I experienced a change in relation to my body that I recognized as having to do with something happening via another body. There wasn't any sense of any "other" energy. There is only one *energy*, so to speak, and the experience of it changes in various circumstances. While you think of yourself as an object, you mistake the myriad expressions of the one "energy" for real differences. When this misconception ceases no energetic differences or "others" are experienced. When I first realized that the sense of "others" had stopped, it was totally amazing to me. Having spent my life seeming to feel "everyone" I could suddenly be in a crowded room and, other than being able to see different bodies, there was no energic experience of *any-one*. Such a relief! (laughing)

Maybe this is another silly question, but is there a difference between the mind and intellect?
Questions are good. I'm sure not so long ago you would never even have thought to ask such questions. It's a sign that you are no longer content with mono-rail thinking.

Coming to conclusions about thoughts is the function of *intellect*. Philosophically, *mind* and *intellect* are considered two of the "coverings" of the Heart. When I first learned this, I asked the exact same question you're asking: "What is the difference between mind and intellect?"

According to the teachings of the great sage Shankara (686-718 A.D.), the intellect relates to the sense of doership—volition or choice. The intellect is considered the faculty of identifying with the bodymind.

I make the distinction that you are identified *as* the bodymind and I am identified *with* it. Either way, that still describes the faculty of intellect. Even though my mind and intellect can be said to be clearer than yours—because I know I'm not the body or any other concept—while mind and intellect are the experience, the relative process is incomplete.

The mental and intellectual "coverings" of the Heart are so transparent now that they no longer concern me. Now the relative ongoing process is the winding down of a habitual way of thinking and acting. The demands and intrusiveness of mind and intellect are winding down.

When the distorted sense of Self first subsided, one could say the intellect went from theory to practice. Before the distortions ceased I had heard Ramesh's explanations and those of Wendell and of other great teachers. They were very helpful to me when all this was still only theoretical. Once theory gave way to practice I found my mind coming up with different imagery and descriptions.

Why did you need anything more in the way of descriptions at that point?
Well, you know how it is when you learn something—anything. You get the teachers' tack on it. When you then start putting it

into practice, it is natural to put your own tack on it. I know in many cases the way in which one's teacher explained everything is the way—after "awakening"—that they continue to teach themselves. But my way of thinking is Western, and my tendency has been to look for Western explanations to the experience—or put it into words that I thought a Westerner could better relate to.

Perhaps this tendency was there because I was teaching before this happened. I don't know. In the past year the imagery my intellect has been coming up with is something I've been putting into writing. At times there was tremendous overwhelm with all this imagery and all these words, but it still carried on coming.

But why do you bother? It seems that now you don't have to think about all these things.

You know how it is when you say, "I don't know why I keep on doing that." You berate yourself for habits and keeping on acting a certain way, but that doesn't make it stop. While you think actions happen because of you, that poses a big problem. You feel guilty, frustrated, confused, or proud.

As much as the writing and all the words seemed overwhelming at times, it was quite clear that it was all happening despite me. Because this understanding is there, there is no censorship or effort to avoid writing. Sometimes I say, "Today I'm going to take a break," that's for sure, but before I know it, there I am at the computer again. That's just what happens. I don't have any say in it.

But what I noticed was that each time I finished a period of writing, there was a further stabilizing that seemed to happen. By coming up with imagery that suited my particular intellect, it seemed as if thoughts and the experiencing of them changed dramatically. Whereas in the beginning there was a constant flow of information booting up in my mind about all of this, that is now changing. Now it comes in spurts, like when I write. But in between times, the mind is less and less of an intrusion. Actually, it's pretty unobtrusive and peaceful most of the time.

Every case is different. In my case, the ongoing relative process of the winding down of thought habits has seemed to go hand in hand with writing.

So are you saying for the process to complete the mind and intellect have to disappear?
Shankara put it beautifully. He talked of, "The mind subsiding into the Heart." Another way of saying this is that the "I" subsides. Because the "I" or personality is identified with via the mind and intellect, when the "I" subsides, it means that which reflected it has also subsided.
Right now I experience *being* via the mind and intellect, in the same way you do. The difference is that my intellect no longer misinterprets this experience to mean, "I am some-body." Self-consciousness is undiluted and my perception of it is no longer distorted.
Manifest-Self is still the orientation. I know I am not this "I" or unique expression of Consciousness but that I am the impersonal functioning of Totality. However, manifest-Self, or the Atman, is still my orientation. Until, if and when, the "I" subsides, the relative process is incomplete.

So "I am" or "I" isn't who we Really are? Ah, I had understood that Self-realization isn't the end of it! You know what I mean.
No. "I am" or "I" is the phenomenal expression of You. Recognizing that the phenomenal expression of you is not contained by, or limited to the body is the first step.
The relative process is broken down into lots of steps, but in a broad sense what is called full Self-Realization is the first "step"—knowing "I am" without the misperception that this "I amness" is the bodymind.
As a so-called seeker, for the longest time I too missed the point; that "I am-consciousness" is not my True nature but my essential, phenomenal nature. I misunderstood Self-realization to be "it" as it were. Later, I began to understand otherwise, but it was really only when the faulty perception of Self ceased that I realized, "This isn't 'it'."

So isn't the sense you have now—"this isn't 'it'"—isn't that frustrating?
No, it's not frustrating. There is just increasing dispassion towards this consciousness and everything else.

153

What do you mean by dispassion? Is that like disinterest?
By *dispassion,* I mean there is a deepening impartiality towards everything. I'd call it a "disconcern." It's not disinterest in the sense of being bored.

The difference is that now nothing external is looked towards as a means of fulfillment. There is a total absence of desires so nothing is considered important. There is no sense of needing to be or feel a certain way anymore.

Dispassion also means "calm," and as dispassion deepens, so does the sense of calm or peace. It's like being the eye of the storm. When the bodymind was identified with, the experience was of being caught up in the storm thinking I had varying degrees of control over it. Then I learned that there was no such thing as control and that everything happened despite me. While this was still an intellectual understanding—and as that understanding deepened—it almost seemed as if the "storm" became more frenetic than ever.

When I began learning, "I am not the body," that was when the coping mode became increasingly difficult to maintain. As the seeking became more intense, it felt as if I was caught up in a huge blender, spinning in circles. Then the misperception of Self fell away and there was a total shift in perception.

For a while, certain tendencies or ways of thinking and acting, were still strong. This is when the sense of calm seemed to fluctuate. I knew experiences couldn't affect Me, but quite a few residual habits of interacting had to fall away before there was a stabilizing. This "stabilizing" is ongoing as dispassion deepens.

Now that many of those tendencies have disappeared, it is like being the eye of the storm and the "storm"—manifestation—doesn't cause a fluctuation in the calm as it used to. No experience feels like a core, all-pervading disruption the way it used to. Because there is dispassion towards all experiences the mind is gradually orienting away from this and that towards the "eye of the storm" or Self and is more and more absorbed by the peace.

It's so frustrating to have an intellectual understanding that I'm not the bodymind and that everything happens despite me. The understanding is there but it doesn't seem to go deeper.

If you're getting really frustrated, it means the understanding *is* going deeper. That is, unfortunately, the way the process goes. First there's complacency and you take your understanding of self at face value. Then you learn that you've had it all back-to-front. You aren't an object, and you don't create your own reality. The more this understanding takes hold, the more frustrated you feel. The frustration keeps you from becoming complacent again. After that, it's just a matter of this new understanding gradually diluting the old ones. The more this happens the more you realize that you understand absolutely nothing. It becomes painfully obvious that you can't understand the non-conceptual You via the conceptualizations of the mind. Unfortunately, the way it goes is that this pain is necessary to keep you awake and not let you buy into any more misconceptions about yourself.

You think so selectively while you are under the delusion that you are some-body. I never realized how selective my thinking was until the delusion stopped. Then I remember the experience I had when my grandfather died back in the 80's. I sat at his bedside and suddenly grieving stopped and I knew with absolute conviction that he had never been born, and hadn't died, and that he had never been this body that was lying in front of me. When I went home to my grandmother she was devastated by the news, but later she said, "I saw light all around you that calmed me so strangely."

Despite this dramatic realization with regard to my grandfather, it never occurred to me to translate this understanding to myself, or others. The thought never came, "Well, if he hasn't been born or died and he isn't the body, perhaps I'm not either." That gives you a pretty strong example of the habit of compartmentalized, selective thinking! (laughing)

You frequently ask us why we are here. I have never really had an answer for this. I wasn't sure what you meant.
It isn't very complicated. I am asking you why you are here. I'm sure you're not here waiting for me to serve you dinner. I'm sure you're not here waiting for me to measure you for a suit. But there are many other *seeming* reasons you can be here. Ulti-

mately you have to be here because you want something from me, and I'm simply asking you what that is?

It isn't that I need to know what you want. It is that **you** need to be absolutely clear on what **you** want. My question will either show you how dispersed your focus is and how many desires you have, or it will show you how single pointed your focus and desire are.

You remain deluded by the fictitious "you" as long as there are desires to control, to own, to avoid, to progress, to attain. Paradoxically, the only thing that can dispel this false notion of self is the desire for the freedom from desires.

I just want to experience being.
Have you ever not experienced being?

No.
So, what's the problem? (laughing)

But I want all the stuff to fall away, the "me" to fall away.
Ah, you are here to get rid of something. (laughing) This "me" you want to get rid of isn't You, it's just a figment of your imagination. This means it isn't real. If something doesn't exist, how can it fall away. The "me" isn't a problem at all. It's your belief that it is a problem that is the only problem. (laughing) I still experience a "me" but I know I'm not it—that it's an illusion—so I have no interest in it at all. It's not a problem.

All I feel is more and more confusion. I just want to know Self; I want to know who I really am.
When confusion is total, it means that whatever you thought you knew has shown itself to be false. When the desire to know Self is total, it means that no other desires remain.

When you desire something and then get it, it isn't the getting that makes you happy, it is the absence of desire that feels so good. Once you understand this, and understand that the illusory self is sustained by desires, all you desire is for the desire to know Self to stop. As the desire for desire to stop grows, so does your sense of confusion.

The false self is always demonstrating pseudo-knowledge—"I know this," "I know that"—so when ABSOLUTE confusion happens it means the illusory self has all but lost it's mesmerizing hold. In total confusion you are at last clear: "I know absolutely nothing." When this confusion is accompanied by ABSOLUTE yearning, and NO other desire remains at all, there is no way the "me" delusion can be sustained.

This is why you must be absolutely clear and one-pointed in your desire, and why I repeatedly ask you, "What do you want?"

Wake up!
Until you open your eyes
You cannot know
That the dream and you
Are unreal.

What?
You don't think You are Dreaming?
Are the dreamed you,
And the dream possible,
Unless You are Dreaming?

Before Dreaming started,
And when Dreaming ends
Who are You?
You must wake up
Before you can answer
This question!

EV

Censorship, Reasons, and Synchronicity

I've been thinking a lot about what you said last time. I was wondering, you say actions and thoughts aren't censored anymore. Surely if you have to plan and choose to act this way instead of that, basically you're censoring one kind of behavior aren't you?

Yes, you are quite right. Making decisions involves a form of censorship.

So that I don't have to continue using cumbersome language I'll use the word *ajnani* when I talk about one who is ignorant of Self.

From the perspective of the ajnani, decisions are thought of as *personal* choices. This is a really weighty belief because when a decision has to be made, you want it to be the "right" one. If it isn't, you think the outcome of that decision is a direct reflection on you. In this way, decision-making is a two-edged sword. On the one hand, it gives you a misplaced sense of power; on the other hand, it poses a potential threat to your self-esteem. This is why, from the ajnani's perspective, decision-making is usually daunting and often involves a lot of effort because self-validation is at stake. From this perspective, decision-making is about trying to *personally* cause a particular outcome.

Lately I get overwhelmed when I have to make decisions, even small ones.

And that might be happening simply because you have too much on your plate and your tired. It's hard to think clearly when you're run down. But, it could be that your self-esteem is in the balance if you believe *you* are the cause of what you experience and the determining factor in how life turns out. That's a heavy trip to lay on yourself and, if that's the case, most decisions are going to seem like a monumental effort.

I get that everything happens despite me, but I guess the habits are still there.
It's just a matter of recognizing the habits for what they are. If you "get" that everything happens despite you, gradually that understanding may start diluting the habits.
The word *censor* comes from the Latin word *censere*, which means to assess. When you force yourself to do something or effort not to do something, it's always because you have made an assessment according to what you think is right or wrong.
The ajnani judges his or her decisions so heavily that *assessment* is rarely practical. The way decisions or assessments are made is a direct reflection of the degree of self-esteem that's there. If you are heavily into guilt and the idea "I create my own reality," then it's very unlikely any decision you make is going to be a practical one because you're making decisions from a place of fear.
Just to remind you, *jnani* means "one" who knows, and basically the "knowing" is of who he is not. In the jnani, guilt and existential fear are absent. This means that assessments are made in a much more practical way. I still weigh up the pros and cons, but whatever the outcome of the decision, I don't think in terms of it being a reflection of me-as-a-person. I know I'm no such concept and that everything happens despite me, so I don't think in terms of right and wrong decisions.

But let's say you decide to help someone invest in the stock market and as a result of your decision they go broke. That won't concern you?
The idea of me helping anyone invest in the stock market *is* pretty disturbing! (laughing) But, kidding aside; of course I'd prefer that that doesn't happen, but if it does I wouldn't berate myself and feel guilty about it. If the decision to help someone invest in stocks happens, it happens despite me. I don't have any real say in either the act of deciding or the outcome.

But relatively speaking you do.
Ah, "relatively-speaking"! (laughing) It's the importance you give to the *relative* that has got you in this whole mess in the first place.
The relative is not real. *Relative* signifies "in relation to," so it is all about the relationships of appearances. Appearances come and go, so they are not real. If you want to know who you *really* are and what is *real*, you have to stop giving importance to appearances.
Relatively speaking, the dynamics of making a decision appear to happen from the standpoint of some-one. When I make a decision, I know *you* haven't made it. I know that the decision happens from the standpoint of my body and not yours. But I also know I am not my body or any other object-identity, so it's quite clear to me that decisions are impersonal actions. Knowing this, I don't have any vested interest in outcome, and I don't worry, "Will I make a right or a wrong decision?" I know that whatever decision happens is the only one that can happen.

So you never feel overwhelmed by decision-making then? That would be great.
I'm not saying there isn't overwhelm sometimes. If physical stress accompanies the process, there can be overwhelm. If I've been writing for fourteen hours straight and have forgotten to eat— which I often do—my body can feel stressed the same way yours does. If I have to make a decision, it can feel overwhelming. The difference is that I don't berate myself for the inability to act as clearly as I might if I were feeling unstressed.

I didn't think you could feel stress?
I still have a physical body made of flesh and blood, and I'm not impervious to it when I overwork and don't take any rest. If I don't get enough rest, as is the case with anyone else, that can lead to stress.

But now it's beginning to sounds as if there are less and less differences before and after Self-realization.

There are as many differences as there are similarities. Remember, *Self-realization* doesn't signify the realization of something that was previously missing. *Self-realization* signifies the realization of who you are NOT.

Let's say I have an inoperable, painful tumor at the time of Self-realization. I'm not suddenly going to stop feeling pain. It's just that I'll experience it fully rather than struggling to avoid feeling it. I won't be thinking, "Why me?" or be feeling sorry for myself. Don't misunderstand. Self-realization doesn't mean you are suddenly impervious to the functions of the body and impervious to your surroundings. On the contrary, you experience them more fully than ever because you aren't battling to maintain or reject any feeling.

Actions are recognized as impersonal because you realize there is no "person" controlling them. Actually, you realize that there is no such thing as control. Everything happens despite you.

At the same time, if I climb a mountain, that action can still feel like an effort in that it involves physical strain to some degree.

But actions still have the appearance of control and intent?
Yes, actions still have the *appearance* of control and intent. If I pick up a glass there is the *appearance* of having had the intent to do so. Once I'm holding the glass, my hand *appears* to be in control of the glass.

In Reality, the act of picking up the glass and holding it happens despite the body and despite any intentions my mind may come up with.

I'm still not clear on the difference between when you make a decision and I make one. You still have to make them it seems, and you can still feel overwhelmed by them.
To give you a better understanding of how it is for me if I have to make decisions, let me give you a hypothetical example. Let's say that I'm physically exhausted and have to spend the evening hosting a party. Probably the only thing I'll want to do is go to bed, and acting charming isn't high on my list of priorities.

So here I have some choices. I can say, "Look I can't stand this, I have to go to bed," or I can let my exhaustion hang out and not be particularly charming, or I can make an effort to stay awake and entertain. You've probably all been in similar situations.

A decision has to be made and I decide to act hospitable and host the party. I go against my feelings of exhaustion and thoughts about it. This tells you that I've made an assessment of the situation and decided to go a certain way. Clearly, this will be a demonstration of *censorship* of what comes naturally to me—going to bed or showing my feelings of exhaustion.

So what's the difference between us doing that and you doing that?

Your essential nature is impersonal functioning. Your essential nature isn't "only functioning in one certain way." The concept of *essential nature* simply signifies *functioning*.

The difference between functioning that happens through your body and functioning that happens through mine, is this: You believe actions happen because of you, and I know they happen despite anyone.

The difference between how you act and how I act is that when I decide to do something and do it, I don't carry on assessing the actions. "Should I have done that instead?" or "Heck, I could have done that better," or "I did that really well!"

If I decided to host a party instead of going to bed, I wouldn't do so all the while thinking, "Phew I wish I'd gone to bed! This is such a drag." There isn't any resignation there.

If during the party I eventually felt more tired than I could stand, I'd probably say, "Sorry, I have to go to bed." Or I might decide to stay awake a while longer, and that decision would again be acted upon without resignation.

But you could decide on something and then re-assess it. Is that what you're saying?

Yes, in exactly the same way you might do. The difference is that, in my case, decisions aren't belabored. There's no guilt in the making of them and no fear or concern about outcome.

But if you were really exhausted, why would you host a party if not out of guilt or the feeling you had to? There always has to be a reason for choosing one thing over another.

The thought might come, "Well, I arranged this two weeks ago and don't want to inconvenience these people by canceling at the last moment," and that *looks* like a reason for sure.

There is usually an *apparent* reason for any choice that is made. This is the case whether I come up with a decision or you come up with a decision. There is usually a multitude of *seeming* reasons for acting this way as opposed to acting another way. The question is: WHY is one reason chosen over another?

It seemed like a better one at the time?

The operative word here is seemed. At the time it seemed like a better reason, but you still don't have any way of telling WHY.

*Well, **my** reason would be that I would feel guilty about letting people down. (laughing)*

That would *seem* like your reason, but you still can't tell me WHY you chose guilt over doing what felt easier. If you are heavily into guilt, it might *seem* that you can't make any other choice, but WHY is that?

I'm heavily programmed I guess.

Why is that? Maybe you'll tell me because of your upbringing, but WHY was your upbringing a certain way? Maybe you'll tell me because your parents had a certain upbringing that colored the way they taught you. Again I'd ask WHY is that?

I don't know.

No action and no event is a stand-alone happening. Everything happens as a synchronized whole. You get up late and rush out of your driveway without looking for oncoming traffic and someone crashes into you. This means that you drop your child of at school an hour after her math exam. This means that she has to stay late and take the exam, etc. etc. etc.

If you would have woken up on time, the person who crashed

into you might not have done so. Your child would have taken her exam. The teacher wouldn't have had to stay late, Etc., etc. When you see the synchronicity of life, it's impossible to pinpoint any one particular reason. When you see the synchronicity of life, you realize the insignificance of *seeming* reasons. Stuff just happens! (laughing)

All we can do is accept what is and learn to go with the flow.
When I talk of accepting or rejecting what is, I'm still talking in terms of acceptance and rejection happening despite you. You can't *learn* to go with the flow, and you can never not go with the flow, because *everything happens despite you!*
Most people think of synchronicity in terms of a harmonious flow of events. The trouble is they fixate on the word *harmonious* and the connotation of synchronicity becomes "everything going the *right* way." That's why the term "out of sync" exists. It describes times when things aren't going how you want them to.
To understand synchronicity in terms of its connotation is as ridiculous as saying, "The only good wave is one that rises and never subsides." Life isn't unchanging. Life is about constant change. Life isn't always *Babes in Toyland*, it has its dark days and traumatic events. Whether the events are lovely or horrible, that's all part of the chain of synchronicity of events.
If something is happening and you seem to reject it, rejection is part of what is. Whatever you are doing is part of that flow, so it isn't a matter of accepting or rejecting. That is just what *appears* to be happening *because* of you. In fact, whatever way you face an event, that's the only way you can face it.
Accepting what is and going with the flow is an idealistic affirmation. It signifies the idea that you have a personal say and choice in what you do. You don't! If something is happening, whatever your attitude towards it, that is part of the flow. This means you are always going with the flow; you can't do otherwise. So don't worry about learning how to do it. You are already doing it, so you can tick that effort off your list! (laughing)

But we have to begin somewhere. If we can begin by at least trying

165

to accept—even if we really know we aren't personally accepting—surely that's a beginning?

What you seem to be saying is, "I understand that there is no such thing as personal effort, but maybe if I begin by making an effort, that's a beginning." (laughing) You can't eliminate rigid beliefs with positive affirmations and actions. It's a start if you don't understand the basic principle—that everything happens despite you. If you understand the basic principle that all actions are impersonal, then that's all that is necessary. As this understanding filters deeper, it does all the work of undermining rigid thinking. As Nisargadatta said, "Understanding is all."

So we just have to be patient then?

You just have to do whatever you are doing or not doing. You can't do otherwise. It's out of your hands. If you understand that, it will gradually or quickly take a lot of pressure off you.

It's one thing to have an intellectual understanding. It's quite another to really know that life is a synchronicity of events.

Don't knock intellectual understanding! (laughing) It's via the intellect that you know about yourself, and it's via the intellect that you have come to conclusions about yourself. It's also via the intellect that you are now investigating the validity of these conclusions.

If you intellectually understand that everything is a synchronistic unfolding, that's a beginning. The way you act may not change instantaneously, but this re-evaluation in your thinking will gradually cause enough disruption to old beliefs that they begin changing.

If you have the intellectual understanding that everything happens despite you, don't you think you'll start looking at life very differently?

Yes, but I'll probably still carry on acting out my role as if I have a say in it.

And that is exactly how I act out roles, AS IF I have a say in them. I don't just sit back when a decision has to be made and say "God do me!" (laughing) I act AS IF I am making the decision, all the

166

while knowing full well that it's being made despite me.

It's not that I even think in these terms or need to affirm this to myself all the time. There is just a deep wordless knowing that supercedes any beliefs I might once have had about control. This knowing is wordless, but it still registers in the intellect as a big relative change.

I used to berate myself and say, "I understand, but it's only an intellectual understanding." Don't think in these terms! The mind and intellect reflect whatever is going on. If you misperceive yourself to be an object but understand otherwise, the intellect reflects these contradictory understandings. A degree of confusion gradually results and, via the intellect, you try to figure this all out. That's why you are here. The intellect is your tool in all this.

Thank you. That helped a lot.

What you need to understand is that how things *seem* and how they *are*, are two very different scenarios. Every event *appears* to have an ultimate reason or cause. If an event has no obvious reason, the usual way is to invent a reason. "It happened so I could learn a lesson," etc., etc. Most everyone likes to think there are reasons behind everything, especially inexplicable events. After all, **unless you can find a reason for everything you feel totally out of control.**

If you have to find a reason for something enjoyable that happens, it's usually because you feel guilty and undeserving or are trying to prove to yourself how deserving you are. This gives you a feeling of control.

Similarly, if a traumatic event happens, you have to find a reason for it. It doesn't matter if the reason you come up with is, "I'm guilty, it's my fault," or, better still (laughing), "It was their fault" or, "It was God's will." As long as you feel the need to give reasons to everything, it is an indication that you fear being out of control.

In the end, if you investigate just a little, you'll discover that it is impossible to find one *ultimate, pivotal* reason for anything that takes place. This is because no event is isolated unto itself.

One event leads to another, which leads to another, ad infinitum.

To find an *absolute* reason for any event is impossible. As it is impossible to come up with an absolute reason, this means that there are no real reasons behind anything that happens. There are relative reasons or causes, but they are *relative* only, not *absolute*.

Can you explain that a bit more?
The word *relative* means the relationship of things to each other. The word *relative* doesn't signify a bunch of things that are autonomous and absolute unto themselves. It *seems* as if relativity is made up of one thing acting independently upon another, but *all* actions are interactions. This is what I mean by how things seem and how they are, are two very different scenarios.
Intellectually you have to understand this before you can begin to understand the invalidity of concepts such as guilt, blame, will-power, and free-will.
"Understanding is all." You just need to understand—intellectually (laughing)—that everything happens despite you, as a part of the synchronicity of Totality.

But if I drive over a nail and my tire goes flat, the reason would be the nail that made a hole in it.
But you don't know WHY you drove over the nail do you? A hundred cars drive down a road and your car happens to drive over the nail. WHY your car and not anyone else's?

Its just coincidence.
What we call *coincidence* means two events that happen simultaneously with no apparent causal connection, or for no discernable reason.
Synchronicity signifies events that occur simultaneously and have mutual impact upon one another, but with no discernible reason.
So *synchronicity* and *coincidence* are really synonymous in that both words signify the absence of a discernible *reason* or cause.
If you, out of a hundred people, drive over a nail and puncture your tire you might decide the reason is that, "It was my destiny," but you really don't know. It is impossible to find an *absolute*

reason for anything, in the same way it is impossible for your mind to come up with *any* absolutes.

You try! (laughing)

So it's all just fate, or destiny?

Ah, another reason! (laughing) Do you see what you are doing in saying that? You are looking for a reason.

Do you understand? It is impossible to know the reason behind anything. It's *absolutely* impossible. (laughing) **You only look for reasons because you want control. As long as you want control you will continue to experience life as a struggle.** As long as you look for reasons, it signifies you are coping and not accepting life as it presents itself.

You want to know "why this happens", "why that happens." If something happens and you are fully experiencing it, you don't ask WHY. The need for reasons for everything denotes your unhappiness with what is.

After all, you wouldn't waste time asking, "Why me?" if you won a million dollars.....at least not until you start feeling guilty or underserving. (laughing) You only look for reasons because you want to feel in control. **As long as you're worrying about finding reasons and having control you are never going to be at peace with yourself.**

You want to create *more happiness in your life and to* let go *of anger.*
You want to come to terms *with grief and* overcome *fear.*
You *believe that peace is only possible once your emotions are "under control."*
And yet you talk of *"having" emotions. You never talk of emotions "having" you.*
So, *what is your problem?*

169

You say, "I want to know
Self."
Who is this "I" that is
Wanting?

The Process of Enlightenment

Are you saying that after enlightenment all experiences are underlain by peace all the time?
There are various stages in the relative process of enlightenment. Remember the word *enlightenment* describes relative change only, nothing real.

Once it is realized who you are not, there is a process of mental adaptation that takes place. The degree to which this adaptation stabilizes determines the degree to which peace is felt. It varies from case to case according to what stage of the process is being experienced.

The word *enlightened* means the absence of prejudice. While you think of yourself as an object, thoughts are extreme. One could say they are highly prejudicial. But as all thoughts are judgments, one might also say that the mind *is* prejudice.

When the primary prejudice, "I am some-body" stops, thoughts are no longer censored, but some extreme thinking may persist. It's more a case of habits, or tendencies, than involvements.

Aren't habits involvements?
Only when there is guilt, fear, or neediness concerning habits can they be said to describe *involvement*. The kinds of habits in my case, the kinds of habits I'm talking about, are ways of thinking that have been going on much of my life, like cultural beliefs for example.

Once the primary involvement—the belief "I am this and that"— ceases, certain habits remain. Because guilt, fear, and neediness are no longer there, these habits gradually wind down.

When an extreme situation arises, a reaction may happen. To the

171

observer it may appear that there is a strong over-reaction, and that may look like involvement. What actually happens is that thoughts and related feelings arise, but because there is no censorship of them, they subside with equal ease. If the situation is extreme, a series of thoughts and related feelings may arise and subside in quick succession. To the outward observer this looks like over-reaction. All that's happening is that there is a series of reactions, but NOT an over-reaction. There is no involvement.

Are you saying that your mind still judges?
All thoughts are judgments because all thoughts are descriptions. My mind hasn't stopped booting up thoughts, so judgment is still there. The difference is that no thoughts are censored, so no judgment is agenda-based. This means there is no involvement. There is no vested interest in avoiding or maintaining any particular situation. Preferences are still there, but they are not rigid. Practical steps are often still taken to remedy a situation, but there isn't any neediness behind them.

While the mind is still full of fears and expectations, you thrash around trying to control each and every experience. Because you believe you are some-body, you think that experiences can affect you. You never stop to ask how the experiencing of anything is possible.

In your waking (and dreaming) states you focus on isolated experiences that change from one minute to the next. You don't look to that which is constant—*experiencing.*

Your essential nature, or manifest appearance, IS Consciousness. Another word for *Consciousness* is *Experiencing.* When the belief, "I am some-body," ceases it is clear that as far as Your essential nature is concerned, all there is Is Consciousness or Experiencing.

Gradually it becomes clear that no experience is more or less important than any other. But this is a gradual process. This is why, in the initial stages, peace is not always deeply felt. It seems to come to the fore when experiences are not extreme and then fall into the background in certain situations. There are many relative changes that take place before peace becomes an abiding experience.

What kinds of changes?
Can you imagine what might happen to your body if you suddenly knew, beyond a shadow of a doubt, that everything happens despite you? Right now you have an intellectual understanding of that, but imagine this understanding permeating your whole
being. There is absolutely no doubt that actions and thoughts
happen despite you. What do you think the experience would be?

Tremendous relief! (laughing)
And how do you think that would affect your experience of the
body and mind?

The body would feel way less stressed. Probably very relaxed.
And the mind wouldn't be going nuts like it is now.
So there you have it! Two dramatic relative changes in body and
mind. Minus stress, the body would function better, health would
improve, and actions would be increasingly effortless. Thoughts
about these changes would come, and the newness of the experience would at first result in a calming of the mind. Then the
mind, totally unused to calm, starts questioning it. The body appears more stressed as a result of the succession of thoughts.
This means that the bodymind is going through a strong adaptation process.
Added to this is the fact that the mind is used to being oriented
towards "you" of all the identities, and that the mind itself was
one of those identities! So periodic disorientation results throughout this whole adjustment. As you can imagine, that would translate into trauma. Fortunately at this point You know you aren't
the body so you don't sit around asking, "Why me?" or feeling
sorry for yourself. Nevertheless, until focus on the bodymind
ceases, total peace isn't a constant experience.
However, as focus increasingly involutes, a stabilizing happens,
and everything starts being experienced from the perspective of
this ever-deepening peace.

I see. So enlightenment—you know what I mean—enlightenment
isn't unending peace and bliss then?

Those words are very deceptive—especially the word bliss.
There are relative stages to enlightenment. First the body and mind are recognized as not You. You no longer identify with age, gender, a name, etc. But cultural beliefs and any very rigid programming that preceded dis-identification from the bodymind, don't disappear immediately. It is clear that they have no bearing or affect on You, but the mind continues to boot them up. The degree to which rigid beliefs were or were not diluted prior to this dictates the dynamics of the enlightenment process.

What do you mean exactly?
I had a certain amount of cultural programming, but because I left England at a very young age, it diluted over the years. My cultural identity hasn't been strong for many years. Added to this, I spent some years investigating beliefs and concepts, and realizing their invalidity. So a certain degree of mental programming remains, but it isn't that strong.

What kind of programming does remain then?
I have to say I'm not really sure. You know how it is when you have been feeling really ill and then the illness abates. You know you felt ill, but it's hard to pinpoint when you started feeling better, and often you quickly forget exactly how ill you felt once you do feel better. When you are feeling "normal" again, it's hard to really recollect what it felt like to feel sick.
It's similar now for me. I realize that life was once experienced very differently. Now experiencing is so natural and effortless, I can't imagine what efforting felt like. I can't even imagine that it ever happened.
When the faulty perception of self falls into perspective, the mind does not immediately lose all rigid beliefs. Although it is clear that agendas are unnecessary, the habit of them can remain. In many cases family bonds, especially with children and spouse, remain strong after enlightenment. Mental conditioning can be very strong with regards responsibility towards those loved ones.
In my case, my main bond is with my husband, John. But he is also in a stage of this relative process. As unusual as I think it is

that this has happened via two bodies that have a strong bond, it makes it much easier. So in John's and my case strong conditioning around our bond isn't there. But John has four children, and the conditioning around the father/child relationship is still there somewhat. That's very natural of course, but in John's case I see that conditioning falling away really fast.

It's very hard to have a perspective on the relative changes. This is because, as programming dilutes, the personality loses rigid definitions that came about with the onset of interaction. Because this process is about losing definition, it's almost impossible to define what changes have occurred, other than retrospectively, and it's even hard to have a retrospective "tack" on all this, because as soon once familiar falls habits fall away, what is left is totally familiar. Clearly, this is because those habits came about through mental conditioning and weren't innate, or natural, to you. So when they fall away, you feel more and more "normal."

The process of enlightenment is rather like learning to surf. Prior to enlightenment, the experience is similar to that of a novice surfer who is simply happy to stay upright as long as he can. The fear of falling flat on your face, or what we call "losing face," is strong. This means that life is experienced as a struggle much of the time.

After enlightenment, it's like becoming a better and better surfer. You don't worry about losing control—because you know there is no such thing—and so it's easier to focus on what is at hand and to do whatever you are doing without expectations or fears.

At first, there is an adaptation process. This is when the sense of peace seems to come and go. Then there is a stabilizing process, and life is *surfed* with an ever-deepening feeling of peace and stability.

Now, in my case, there is still identification *with* the body, mind, and personality, but I know that I am not these, or any other concept. I identify *with* them, but not *as* them. I know that Consciousness or Experiencing is my essential nature or manifest appearance. As long as I am oriented towards this body and personality called "Esther," the process of enlightenment is incomplete.

175

So you are still identified with something?
Yes, I am still identified with the body, but not in the sense that you are. You think you *are* the bodymind. I know that I am not this concept, but the knowing of this concept happens in relation to this body and personality called "Esther."

But if there is any kind of conditioning, then you'd have to say there is prejudice, wouldn't you?
Yes, you would.
Intellect describes the aspect of mind that reflects the personality in the word "I." *Intellect* is also the aspect of mind that interprets the body in terms of "mine." When the mind ceases booting up the misinterpretation "I am some-body," the intellect continues reflecting the unique expression of Consciousness happening through the body in terms of "I." At this point it is clear that You are not this "I," but it is still apparent, and so there are thoughts about it—and we can call these thoughts *prejudice*. The prejudice isn't dogmatic as before, but it's still a form of prejudice.
When the realization happens that You aren't an object, the concept of ownership shows itself to be completely invalid. Despite this understanding, the intellect continues to reflect the relationship between that particular personality and body in terms of "mine." This means that there are still thoughts about ownership, even if they are understood from a very different perspective.
Because there are still thoughts about "I" and "mine"—even though they are now in clearer perspective—it means there is still prejudice. Again, it isn't dogmatic, needy prejudice, but it must still be called prejudice.
Relatively speaking, a huge shift in perspective has happened when you realize who you are not. This shift in perspective is often termed *enlightenment*. However, *enlightenment* means the absence of prejudice. It doesn't mean *less* prejudice. And at this stage it must be said there is still prejudice—albeit minus the rigidities that were there before. This means that the process of enlightenment is incomplete.
Relatively speaking, a shift in perspective has happened that is huge in comparison to the perspective that preceded it. In com-

paring ignorance of self to this perspective one can say a degree of enlightenment has happened.

Relatively speaking, this *degree* of enlightenment is a quantum leap in perspective. That is why when you are in the presence of the guru who embodies this perspective, it can have tremendous impact on you. That is, if your perspective is still limited to thinking in terms of "I am a lump of flesh and bones with an attitude and will-power." (laughing)

But are you saying that this isn't really enlightenment as long as there's prejudice? Or are you saying there are degrees of enlightenment?

In reality, there is no such thing as enlightenment. Enlightenment is just a relative term describing relative changes in perspective. Because *enlightenment* describes something relative, it is measurable. So from a relative standpoint, yes, one could say there are degrees of enlightenment.

But how could one function if the personality stopped being identified with?

No "one" has ever functioned. There has always only been impersonal functioning. If you watch someone sleeping, they may toss and turn, even talk in their sleep or sleep-walk. Some people even go to the refrigerator and prepare and eat meals for themselves in their sleep. The *person* is totally unaware of any action, and is unaware of him or herself, but functioning still happens.

In my case the personality is still identified *with*, even though I know "I" am not it. So I cannot talk from direct experience about these dynamics. My sense is that second-nature functions continue as before. However, this would probably mean that there is a certain physical vulnerability. My understanding is that the Satguru is usually cared for by others at that stage.

Shankara expresses it this way; that the bodymind and the rest of manifestation is to the Subject what your shadow is to you. There is awareness of it, but it is of no concern.

So you're saying that deep sleep is what we should aim for!
(laughing)

177

Well, you go to bed tonight and *aim* for deep sleep. (laughing) Lie there and focus really hard on trying to fall into deep sleep. Either you'll find it impossible to sleep because your mind is struggling so hard, or sleep will happen. Either way, what use has the struggle been?

Okay, I see. So conditioning is just going to remain until it goes. There's no point in doing anything to get rid of it.
Certain techniques might seem to help the process of diluting conditioning. For example, I write and the formulation of words that are put into writing appears to help the diluting process. It's not that there is heavy conditioning where I'm concerned, but as long as thought-prejudices remain at all, the process is incomplete.

As far as you are concerned, it doesn't matter what techniques you try. You don't have a choice in your decision. If you do certain techniques, you do them. If you don't, you don't. You have absolutely no say in any of this.

It isn't a matter of doing nothing, but it also isn't a matter of avoiding doing anything. You can't deliberately avoid doing something and you can't deliberately decide to do something. You are just going to continue doing whatever you are doing. It may look as if certain techniques are helping dissolve rigid programming. But if they are dissolving, it's probably because they were ready to dissolve anyway and the technique simply coincided to anchor those changes.

Are you saying therapies and techniques and coming here really have nothing to do with relative changes?
What I'm trying to communicate is that whatever is needed will happen. If you put too much store in any technique, it risks becoming a crutch. Hanging out on the beach and relaxing may be just as beneficial in certain cases as going to seminars and sitting in uncomfortable positions. It is unimportant what you do because you can only do what you are doing. No activity is more or less important than any other. It just looks that way while you are in efforting, controlling mode.

It's hard to understand that conditioning remains once you realize you aren't the body or the mind.

Yes, this is why it has happened so often that disciples of certain teachers have become disenchanted. The teacher may have held rigid beliefs about celibacy prior to enlightenment. After enlightenment, even though he knows no effort is necessary, he may continue to teach from the standpoint of the belief that celibacy has spiritual benefits.

For the belief in celibacy to have arisen, it was probably engendered by guilt and strong ideas about sex being unspiritual or distracting.

Once enlightenment happens, teachings may still continue regarding the benefits of celibacy. But because guilt is no longer there, beliefs in its value will gradually lose their hold. Then what often happens is that sexual expression—that was previously curtailed and censored—begins to surface. The teacher is then seen to act in direct contradiction to his own teachings.

This is very confusing and disturbing to his disciples. But one could say that the teacher is most useful to them at that point. This is because he's offering them such a clear mirror of their own issues around sexuality. Unfortunately, there is usually so much blame going on—towards the teacher—that this opportunity is missed.

It sounds as if there is still a learning process going on for the teacher then?

Actually it's not a learning process, but an un-learning process, or a neutralizing process. So it's really a continuation of the first stage—from ignorance of Self to knowing, or from ajnana to jnani. If prior to enlightenment rigid physical disciplines and strong cultural beliefs were adhered to, they may not disappear instantly. After enlightenment, when that conditioning is triggered and surfaces, the underlying peace I talk about may be somewhat masked. If conditioning around a relationship is still strong—such as ideas on raising children—when that conditioning arises, the peace is periodically masked. That is, mental conditioning becomes the orientation. The process of enlightenment is about a re-orientation away from the perspective of duality in relation to the "I" or unique expression of Consciousness happening through a particular body.

As we're talking about enlightenment, I won't keep on prefacing the term with explanations. But do remember, the word simply describes relative changes—seeing the false self for what it is. Enlightenment doesn't mean anything has happened to any "one." Now, for example, in some cases the "path" prior to enlightenment involves a physical discipline such as hatha yoga, or a dietary discipline, or a meditation discipline. If this is the case, the beliefs about the benefits of that discipline will probably be strong. Even though, after enlightenment, it's clear that no discipline is necessary—what happens just happens—the programming about its value may remain.

But why would there be concerns about physical or dietary disciplines if You Know you aren't the body?
I know I'm not the body, but a certain amount of conditioning is still there about what disrupts its health. I still enjoy cigars, especially when I write, and there are still fleeting thoughts about cigars being bad for the health. Although I certainly wouldn't say I am in any way "worried sick" about it.

Isn't that necessary though? I mean, you have to stay healthy, and if you don't care for the body....?
I would have to say that rigid dogmatic beliefs and fanaticism are way more detrimental to the health of the body than anything else. Surveys have been done on various people from different cultures and they show that what you think about your food dramatically affects the way the body absorbs nutrition from it. For example, if you think of hamburgers as junk food and bad for you, your body will probably not benefit greatly from them. Whereas if you believe hamburgers are a good source of nutrition, your body is more likely to benefit from them. There is so much guilt around food nowadays that it's not surprising that people have so many digestive disorders.

As far as I am concerned, I feel it's helpful if the body stays healthy. I certainly don't want to be a burden to anyone because of ill health. But "I" am not going to be affected by the body's condition. Even if the body "dies," it's of no concern to Me. But, like you, I'd probably prefer that the body "dies" of old age. I'd prefer that to having it squished under a truck or riddled with painful cancer.

So the body still feels pain?
No! The body is oblivious to pain. The body has never felt anything! The body is an appearance in Awareness. The contrast that happens gives rise to "I am-consciousness" in relation to the body. When any form of experiencing happens it is of this consciousness, NOT the body.

But if you cut a finger, it bleeds. If you eat too much, the stomach bloats and feels uncomfortable....
Consciousness is the animation of the body. You cut a finger and it bleeds. This is a product of that animation. Your stomach bloats, and this animation is also due to Consciousness. The body is, and always has been, an inanimate object, animated by Consciousness! The body is no different to a glove puppet without a hand in it. Consciousness is the hand, as it were, that animates the body. The body doesn't feel this animation.
Seeing, feeling, hearing, and smelling are attributed to the sense organs. These organs don't have any experience whatsoever. They are inanimate objects animated by consciousness—the manifest expression of You. Do you "get" that?

Yes, but the mind still has thoughts about what you see and feel and experience?
No! The mind doesn't have thoughts. The mind doesn't experience thoughts. The mind is thoughts, a whole parade of them. The mind is a reflection of the animating principle—You. Only You, the animating principle, can be said to have and experience thoughts. The body does not cause it's own animation, and cannot feel it. The mind doesn't cause it's own animation, and cannot think or experience thoughts.

If something is caused by a factor other than itself, how can it take over and start causing and feeling?

Out of the non-dual, non-manifest Absolute, the dualistic appearance of Self was "born." This phenomenon describes *Self-effulgence*, which means something that illuminates or animates itself. You, who You Really are, is Self-effulgent, Self-animating.

You, the Absolute, are prior to the appearance of the body. The body is subject to "birth" and "death" so it is not an absolute. How can something that does not cause itself, such as the body and mind, suddenly begin to act upon itself?

It can't.

You see, it doesn't take much simple deduction to understand that your perception of self is faulty. The "birth" of the body happened despite you. You didn't cause or have any control over this *happening*. And yet you think that once the body is "born," suddenly control of it is in your hands. Ridiculous, eh?

Yes.

The body and mind are the receptacles via which experiencing is possible. They don't in any way experience anything themselves. The body doesn't feel, and the mind doesn't think. Are you with me?

Yes.

Good. (laughing) While you are identified with the bodymind, experiencing is attributed to the body and mind objects. But in fact, You *are* the Seeing, Hearing, Smelling, Thinking. The essential, manifest expression of You-the-non-manifest *is* Experiencing or Consciousness.

Ah.

If, right now, that understanding went beyond the mind, the shift would be reflected in the cessation of extreme, prejudicial thoughts. Temporarily, as a result of this shift in your thinking processes, you would probably experience a degree of peace. That *degree* of peace is relative to how you felt before.

In my case, prejudice is no longer dogmatic, and because mental conditioning continues to dilute, my experience is of an ever-deepening sense of peace. I can't say that I experience absolute peace, however. This is because thought-prejudices still remain, and as long as any kinds of judgments are being made, *absolute* peace isn't going to be the experience.

But you still experience a lot more peace than we do?
I don't know what you experience. I just know that my experience of the body and mind, before I stopped thinking I was them, is radically different from the present experience. It's very hard now to recall exactly how I felt before, but my sense is that focus was very externalized much of the time. Even though by nature I was fairly introspective, I'd say that focus was superficial.
Now the experience is almost of being right in the back of the audience watching whatever is going on. The body feels totally relaxed all the time and the mind is only busy when it needs to be. The rest of the time thoughts come and go, but the mind is very peaceful unless I have to think about something in particular such as planning or deciding something. So, relatively speaking, the change is dramatic.
For a while, when the body became stressed for one reason or another, the peace dissipated somewhat and some physical tension would be there. Now I really don't even experience that happening. The physical stress might be there in the sense that I know I have to lie down or stop working for a while. I can't say there is tension as before. There really isn't any tension, just a sense of needing to re-vitalize the body, which happens very quickly.

That sounds amazing.
I used to live on nervous energy. Now my nature is still to undertake most anything I do with tremendous speed. John says it feels like a tornado is hitting when I start cleaning the house. But, as strange as it sounds, even tremendous physical effort happens from a very peaceful *place*.

That sounds like absolute peace to me, but you're saying it's not absolute?

As long as duality is experienced via a dualistic object—in my case, one called Esther—there is prejudice. Preferences are there, even if they aren't strong. Thoughts about Esther in relation to the world are still there, even though they are void of worry, fear, guilt, or any of those involvements. As long as there are thoughts there is not *absolute* peace.

When duality ceases being filtered through the intermediary objects of mind, intellect, body, and personality—the combination of which is called "I"—then prejudice is completely absent.Only from this totally objective standpoint—minus any involvement at all—can *absolute* peace be the experience.

*It sure feels like I've got a long way to go before I even experience **relative** peace.* (sigh)

Right now you are beginning to "get" that you aren't who you think you are. Some changes in attitude are happening, and old conditioning is being questioned. This means that that conditioning is already on shaky ground. If, or when, your investigation intensifies, the intensity of it will begin to shake more and more of those old thinking patterns loose. When this starts happening, it means the process of enlightenment is underway. That is, a degree of light is being shed on ignorance of Self. When sincere seeking gets fully underway, the process of enlightenment is underway.

First the falling away of rigid prejudices must happen. When the primary dogmatic prejudice—"I am some-body with will-power"—subsides, the mirror of mind catches the light of Consciousness in a much more direct way.

What do you mean?

Light cannot be seen. You only ever see the objects that are illuminated by it. Let's say you make two tiny holes in an empty sealed box. You make these holes directly opposite one another and you shine a bright beam of light, directing it so that it shines directly out through the opposite hole without hitting the inner surfaces of the box. Then you make a third hole in the box, being careful not to allow any light to seep through it into the box. If you were then to look through this third hole, still not letting light permeate it, you would only see darkness. As the strong beam isn't hitting any object or surface within the box and is exiting directly out of the hole on the other side, nothing is illuminated. This is what I mean by, you can't see light; you only ever see the objects it illuminates.

And as you know, you can't see objects unless they are illuminated. Because you have the experience of objects, it means something is illuminating them. Before the appearance of manifestation, there would have to have been no-thingness or the non-manifest. The non-manifest, because it is—as the words imply—not an object, would not be subject to light.

Within the non-manifest, non-dual Absolute manifestation has appeared. This means that within the absence of light, light has appeared—because objects or appearances cannot be perceived unless something illuminates them.

The question is, how does light appear in darkness? The only solution to this question is that "darkness" has illuminated it-Self. That makes no sense, so it isn't really a solution to this riddle. However, it does give you one more indication that via the mind you can't know anything about the Truth.

Before the appearance of manifestation, the Absolute was unaware of it-Self. Another word for Self-awareness is Consciousness. This means that Consciousness is the "light" of the Absolute. The mind-object picks up this light and reflects it in the thought "I am."

In the newborn infant this "light" isn't being directed towards the body and so the sense "I am" is actually wordless. When thoughts begin to form, it is because the body, and other objects, are being picked up in the reflector or the mirror of mind, and the reflection the mind holds is distorted. This distortion results in the thought "I am some-body."

When it is realized that you are not any-body, it means that the mind has become a clearer reflector of Consciousness. Strong prejudice towards the body has fallen away and, minus this involved focus, the light of Consciousness—"I am"—is picked up more clearly. We could then say that a strong degree of enlightenment has happened. Here *enlightenment* signifies that the mind is a more direct receptor of the light of Consciousness. Involvement has subsided to a large degree which means the mind is, so to speak, orienting away from the illusion towards Self.

But the mind can't know Self!
The mind can't *know* anything. The mind is simply a refracting mechanism. It refracts the light of Consciousness and the objects of manifestation illuminated by that "light". These *refractions* are what we call thoughts.

The more deeply it is realized that the mind holds no Truth, the more focus orients away from manifestation towards the light of Consciousness or Self. The mind becomes increasingly "absorbed" by the light of Self. In rare cases, when this shift in orientation is total, the light of Self fully absorbs the "I" thought.

Once this *happens* the light of Consciousness is no longer deviated via one particular aspect of duality and subjective *knowing* subsides into objective Knowledge or absolute objectivity.

This *shift* in perspective is what is called "full-enlightenment" but that is a description of a <u>relative</u> change only. As such it has no bearing on Reality; no bearing on the Truth.

Focus on the concept of *enlightenment* only serves to perpetuate the habit of expecting and hoping and what you are hoping for isn't real. The "person" to whom you attribute the act of hoping isn't real. When you have total clarity on this the illusion will end and as it is an illusion it has never *really* existed. This means that in Reality nothing will have happened! In other words: **there is no such thing as enlightenment!** (laughing)

The Frustrated Seeker

I have spent years in this search. I understand, as you say, that enlightenment is a relative term, but as a so-called seeker it's hard not to think about it. (laughing) Is it just a matter of Grace? Is that how you see it?

When it's said, "Enlightenment happens by Grace," it's another way of saying that enlightenment happens despite you. When I suddenly fully "got" that I wasn't the body, I certainly attributed it to Grace because at that stage there was still *some-one* experiencing all this. Some identities were still strong and the concept of the Divine as separate to me had not fully subsided, so there was tremendous gratitude. At that time I could only think in terms of Grace.

Another term that is often used to mean *Grace* is, "*It is God's will.*" The trouble is that as soon as you hear the word *Grace* it's almost impossible not to think of being graced by someone or something separate to you. It's the same with the words, "It's God's will"; it is almost impossible not to register the implication that God is an entity separate to you.

These words—*Grace* and *the will of God*—are often used in the context of teachings that make it quite clear that there is no separate *God* and that everything happens spontaneously. But for many it's hard to break free of mental conditioning, especially where separateness and personal doership are concerned. Until that conditioning is totally broken down such evocative concepts as *Grace* and *God's will* can often perpetuate these beliefs.

"Thy will be done," and "It's God's will" have been very helpful understandings for me though.

187

Yes. When it is really understood or deeply intuited what these words mean—that there is no personal will—there are few words that can have greater impact on a life. The trouble is, most people pray, "Thy will be done," and in the same breath ask God to give them this or that. That's like saying, "Do what You want, but can You make the outcome one that I'll like?" I always had a problem with this prayer, even as a child. I figured, "If God's will is always being done anyway, why should I pray 'Thy will be done?' Am I telling God it is okay with me if He or She acts how He or She wants to?" It didn't make much sense to me.

I never thought of *God* as someone up in the clouds; I never thought of God as a person. Even as a child I just figured God was an all-pervading energy that was more powerful than me. In that context, I prayed to this energy thinking I needed to put it out there that I was up for any challenge. As "Thy will be done" didn't make sense to me, my prayer was, "Whatever it takes." I guess it was as much a motto as a prayer.

I always tended to add the most horrific scenario to this prayer, such as, "Whether I lose a limb, am paralyzed, or go blind." I guess if I'd known about neurotoxic fish poisoning, that would have been right up there on my list. (laughing)

When I read Ramana and Ramesh, the words, "Thy will be done," made deeper sense to me in terms of: "Everything happens despite me." But the impulse was still there to pray in some way, although I understood there was no "other."

I don't tend to talk about *Grace* or *God's will* because I feel they are concepts that can perpetuate confusion. At the same time I don't discard these concepts as serving a very good purpose in shifting certain people's understanding.

My sense is that in perhaps a majority of people throughout the world there has always been a strong instinct towards prayer—be it to an idol, nature, a God or Gods. Instinctively the sense is there that there is a greater power than the pseudo-self. Sometimes it takes a life-threatening situation before a person gets in touch with this sense. In other cases I feel prayer is a strong, inborn instinct. And by *prayer* I mean *giving thanks* rather than begging for something.

Unfortunately, dogmatic religious teachings about *sin* have distorted this intuited sense of a Higher Power than the "me." When it is taught, "God made man in His image," it's easy to conclude that God must be judgmental because people are judgmental. This belief then causes an even deeper sense of separateness, not only from God but from ones fellow man. You just have to look at the different religions and how teachings that were once very clear have been distorted by dogma. As a result the different religious factions find themselves warring, accusing and judging; causing an ever-greater rift between peoples.

Most religions advocate humility with regard to God, but selective thinking blinds people. The idea that humility is something to exercise also towards one's fellow man doesn't seem to occur to a lot of people.

I guess to most people humility sounds like weakness. It's hard to act humbly, especially in our competitive society.

Most people interpret the word *humility* to mean the absence of opinions and that's why it seems like an impossible virtue. It is one thing to be goal-oriented and competitive and to steam-roll everyone else's opinions in order to attain your goal. It is quite another matter if you have an inspired vision, and to be open-minded enough to listen to other people's attitudes along the way.

Motivation is always goal-oriented and usually gives rise to competitive behavior. Inspired visions may seem to be no different, but they are always accompanied by a deeply intuited sense that nothing can get in their way. That's why the true visionary usually displays humility and the ability to be open to other people's ideas. Then, even if the vision isn't realized, that same humility carries them through until another vision arises.

The competitive go-getter has a very hard time with the concept of humility. This isn't so much because it's hard to act with humility. It's more a case of it being hard for people to get beyond the idea that *humility* signifies abject submission. That connotation certainly is hard for most people to come to terms with. It really is a misinterpretation of what the word *humility* signifies.

To the visionary, the words "Thy will be done" are probably easier to grasp. To the competitive personality, "Thy will be done" is usually only used in the context of how well *God's will* fits in with their own expectations.

I guess the word humility did have pretty derogatory connotations for me. That helps a lot.

You say that who we think we are, is an illusion. But you also said there was some-one feeling gratitude in the first stage. That sounds as if you are contradicting yourself.

While you mistake Self to be *some-one,* you think in terms of owning and losing. This is because objects are subject to gain and loss. This is why you experience gratitude when you "gain" a good experience and displeasure when you feel you are missing out.

Because I hadn't fully disidentified from the false self I called *some-one,* gratitude was felt. When that aspect of the illusion, the some-one, was fully recognized as false, the sense of gratitude ceased.

Who or what You really are has never been *any-body* or *any-one.* These words refer to the illusory "you," and *illusion* simply means faulty perception. By "*some-one* feeling gratitude," I am referring to this faulty perception only. Is that clearer?

Yes.

When the illusory "you" starts being recognized for what it is—not You—it is usually a gradual process. I guess one could liken the process to a method actor who can only come out of character gradually. He knows the character he's been playing isn't him, but for a while he has difficulty not acting out certain traits that belonged to his stage persona. Similarly there are habits that have to wind down before you fully recognize you aren't a gender, name, age, role, etc.

And remember, I'm talking about a relative happening only. The mirage of a pool of water in the desert does not wet the sand.

Similarly, the mirage of you-the-person has not altered or affected You in any way. This means that nothing has really happened. All I'm talking about are relative happenings, nothing real.

I get that, but we still experience the relative and so we think in terms of that. As a seeker, it's hard not to think something has to happen. Listening to you it's hard not to think that something happened.

The relative isn't something that can be ignored, of course. The trouble is you have spent your life mistaking relativity for Reality. It's hard to get beyond the idea that *enlightenment* is something real that happens to the pseudo-you.

Enlightenment simply describes the realization that who you *thought* you were has never been You. Just because you think you are a lump of flesh and bones, and waste products with an attitude, this hasn't changed You in any way. If you realize that You aren't this object, this realization won't change You either. So nothing really happens, and *nothing* has ever really happened to You.

But it's very hard to really "get" that when you're still desperately seeking! (laughing)

I know it is. Even if you understand that everything happens despite you and that you are not an object, until the mental conditioning disappears fully, certain concepts are easy to latch onto.

As this was my experience, I tend not to use certain concepts. I don't use a lot of phrases that my teachers used with me. This doesn't mean their words weren't very beneficial to me. But in the end it was primarily the energy behind the words that unglued my rigid thinking processes. The words themselves played a strong initial role in throwing my mind off track, but ultimately words play only a very small role in this process.

It just seems to me now, "Why introduce *any* concepts that seem unnecessary?" Why give your minds anything to latch onto that can keep you locked in habitual thought processes?"

When I'm here, it feels as if the words aren't important. Much of the time I don't even seem to hear the words.
That's right. The words are unimportant because the communing is really non-verbal. Even if you are not with the teacher but reading their words, it's the energy behind the words—even then—that does most of the work.

Different people are at different stages in this unraveling process. Initially some people have a lot of strong, rigid opinions when they come here. That's why I avoid using certain terms, because I don't want to give them more concepts to latch onto. Others of you *experience* the teachings rather than hear the words; but for some, words need to be dealt with first before this can happen.

All teachings are to a degree colored by the unique intellect via which they happen. In my case, the words *Grace* and *God's will* described the feeling of being blessed that I had since a tiny child. But later on in life, I found that these concepts, like any concepts, could easily perpetuate rigid thought habits in me. So I guess that's why I don't tend to use these words very much here.

Let's face it, your minds can only latch onto concepts, and I can only speak in concepts. But I try to break them down as I go, to invalidate them as I go. Relatively speaking, the terms *Grace* and *God's will* are useful when it comes to understanding, "Everything happens despite you." They are perhaps not so beneficial in that they can perpetuate the belief that there is a separate Power.

But the "me" is not that Power.
The terms *God* or *Higher Power* relate to That which is NOT the pseudo-self or "me." In that sense you are correct in saying the "me" is not that Power. In the sense I am talking, the "me" is part and parcel of the phenomenal reflection of that *Power*.

The "me" is just a bundle of thoughts that have been attributed to the sense "I am." As a result, the experience of *being* is distorted and you experience being some-body. This hasn't changed You in any way, but it has given rise to the sense of separateness you feel.

Your essential nature is *Experiencing* or Consciousness. Your essential nature is impersonal, effortless acting and effortless doing. Even if you think actions happen *because* of you—and this makes them seem like personal struggling—they are still happening spontaneously. Seeming struggling is still spontaneous. This means that your essential nature is never obscured. Your perception of Your essential nature is merely distorted.

But isn't that the same thing—distorted and obscured? I mean, if I throw paint on top of a painting the original painting is both distorted and obscured.

While there is a body via which you experience being the sense "I am" never changes. It looks as if it changes when you think in terms of "I am now this and I'm going to be that." But these seeming changes don't cause the sense "I am" to disappear and you are always aware of being. Even when you've been in deep sleep and know you were unaware of yourself, this knowing is retrospective. This means that you never have the experience of not knowing you are. It's only because you focus on the descriptions you have added to this sense that you think Self is hidden from you.

But we still experience inhibitions and put up fronts as long as we think we are the body. That does seem to hide the Self. If it didn't, surely we wouldn't be seeking so desperately?

When I was a child, I remember that my grandmother was always losing her glasses. She would often say, "I'll give you five francs if you can find them." Once I had secured her promise, I used to scurry around for a while pretending I was looking for them. Then I'd triumphantly grab them off her nose and say, "I've found them! Now can I have my five francs?" It worked every time. I used to laugh at her, but now that I do the exact same thing myself, I am happy not to have such a little tike of a granddaughter.

Your search for Self is really just like that. Although actions appear inhibited, and you feel these inhibitions are "yours," they are still happening spontaneously and impersonally—despite you. As Your essential nature *is* spontaneity, it hasn't changed just because it *appears* to be inhibited.

When I recognized the identities as not Me, I remember it hit me that another word for essential nature is EXPERIENCING. I'd heard the word Consciousness over and over, but I just hadn't "got" what was being said.

All the way through the search, I found it necessary to put things into my own words. Afterwards, I found I was still doing that, so now instead of Consciousness I tend to use the word *experiencing* to describe *essential nature*.

Through different bodies different experiences are had, but *experiencing* is unaffected by any of them.

You give various labels to *experiencing* according to what is going on in your life and how you react to different experiences. As the saying goes: "A rose by any other name would smell as sweet." *Experiencing* by any other name is still Experiencing. Whether it is given the name struggling or fearing it is still *experiencing*. This is why I say, "your perception of Self is distorted but manifest-Self is not obscured in any way."

But our essential nature has to be obscured as well as distorted, otherwise we wouldn't be seeking so hard, would we? I still can't see how you can make this differentiation.

In deep sleep you don't know experiencing isn't happening, do you? You only know about the cessation of experiencing once you wake up and experiencing recommences. This means that you are never directly aware of the cessation of experiencing.

Whether you call it "I am-consciousness," or *experiencing*, these words describe Your essential nature. Whether the pseudo-self is identified with or not, experiencing is still given various names. I still say, "I am thinking," "I am eating," etc. If I have to carry a very heavy object I might say, "I am struggling with this damn thing."

Just because I give *experiencing* different names, or just because you give *experiencing* different names, doesn't change it. Just because it is perceived in different ways doesn't mean it is hidden.

A *prism* is what we call a ball of glass covered in facets. This doesn't stop the ball of glass from being glass. The facets of a prism don't hide the glass. They just change the appearance of the glass.

Similarly, whether experiencing takes on the appearance of *thinking, worrying,* or whatever it is still experiencing. Experiencing is no more hidden from you than it is from me. I know that experiencing is impersonal. You think you are an object *having* personal experiences. Either way, experiencing is going on and continues to be *experiencing.*

This is what I mean by "your essential nature is not hidden from you." Your essential nature is no more hidden from you than mine is from me. It's just that the perception of Your essential nature has been distorted because you think you are an object having personal experiences that can affect you.

All that has to happen is that you recognize the distortions for what they are. Once this conviction happens totally—if it does—you will continue attributing labels to experiencing. The knowing will be that no experiences affect You. Because nothing affects or changes You in any way, the struggle to maintain this experience, or avoid that experience ceases. Practical steps are still taken to effect change, but there is no fear or agenda as far as the outcome is concerned. Each outcome is dealt with in the same way—minus fear, minus desire.

Let's say you see a piece of rope and think it's a snake. The rope isn't hidden, is it? It's just that your perception of it is distorted. Once you know for certain that the rope isn't a snake, it doesn't matter what appearance it takes on, your conviction doesn't waiver.

Ah, okay. Now it's making more sense.

I understand I'm not an object. I understand everything happens despite me. I understand that there is no seeker; that the seeker is the Sought. But as far as I'm concerned, all there is is frustration! I understand, but I still keep on buying books and coming to Satsang and sitting at home feeling totally frustrated.

Ah, that was my exact same lament. (laughing) When I read Nisargadatta's words—over and over again— "Understanding is all," it both helped and frustrated me, just as you are frustrated. I kind of understood what was meant, but all I could think was "If 'understanding is all' and IF I understand this clearly, why do I still experience the frustration of not knowing Self? Why do I still experience limitation and guilt and all of that? Where is this damn Self?"

It doesn't matter how clear it is to you that You are not an object and "there is no seeker." You have spent a lifetime relating to object-identities, so it's hard to get beyond the idea that Self will be experienced in the same way as any other identity.

You say you understand that the seeker is the Sought, but if you really understood, the search would stop instantly. The trouble is you think in terms of "the Sought" as being something you will feel in the same way you feel your identities. ,

Lately all I feel is empty. Whether it is in relation to my wife or anything else, I just feel emptiness. I don't feel it all the time, but I guess depression would be the best word for it.
What desires do you have?

I used to have lots of desires. Actually, I thought that I still had one desire and that was to have a boat. I always dreamed of having a boat. Now that I have the chance to have one, I find I'm not even interested in that. All I desire is for all this to fall away or end.
IF all other desires have ceased it means that the pseudo-you has lost most of its thunder. The false "you" is desire-based, or made up of desires. You want this and then that, and all these desires stem from the desire to control.

I know there is no such thing as control. I feel totally out of control.
Okay. You know there is no such thing as control. You say you have no desires but the desire for all this to end. By "all this," I imagine you mean the "me"?

Yes.
The "me," in the way you now think of it, is basically nothing more than a bunch of desires related to different identities, and

the need to control them and the world you interact with. You say that you are clear that there is no such thing as control, and all desires have fallen away apart from the desire for the remaining desire to fall away. Is that it? (laughing)

Yes. That's it exactly. I desire to stop desiring anything! (laughing)

Perhaps that is the case, and all that remains is the desire to stop desiring. IF this is so, it would be helpful to investigate this last desire.

This desire is not strongly related to objects, is it? It is basically the desire to know Self—a non-object. But as long as there is desire, it is because you believe something is missing. After all, you don't desire something you know you have, do you?

To a degree, you understand that YOU are not missing. At the same time you experience not knowing Your Self. It feels like a ridiculous, frustrating dilemma I know.

The good thing is that at last you understand that You are not an object. You also understand that there is no object to seek. If a non-object is seeking a non-object, what does this equation add up to? What is left if a non-object is seeking a non-object?

"Me-the-frustrated-seeker!" (sigh)

Listen again. If you know you are a non-object, and you know that you seek a non-object, what remains that you can identify or put a word to?

Seeking. Desiring. Feeling frustrated! (laughing)

Deduct the seeker-object and the Sought-object and what you are left with is *Seeking.*

Seeking is the description you now give to *Experiencing. Desiring* is the description you now give to *Experiencing.* Identification with the labels *desiring* and *seeking* is ongoing as long as you attribute them to the "me" identity. This is why you say, "I am the frustrated seeker."

All you have to understand is that Your essential nature is still being misinterpreted. Your perception of Your Self is distorted.

You feel emptiness and call it *depression*. I remember the sense of emptiness was overwhelming to me. My mental interpretation of it was also *depression*.

It took me the longest time, spinning in circles in this emptiness trying to make head or tail of it before I "got" that what I was experiencing wasn't an illness. The emptiness was so unfamiliar because I had spent my life filling it with identities. When those identities began losing their hold it was the most alien feeling. I just didn't feel like myself anymore. Gradually I began to understand that this was because what I called "myself" had all but disappeared.

The trouble was I had expected to feel wonderful if this happened, but all I felt was this terrible emptiness. It felt dreadful. (laughing)

It took a while before I realized that "the Self" was absolutely nothing like any identity. For want of better words, I began to realize: "I am the emptiness." That is, I realized the emptiness was the absence of personalized identities.

Before that I had the intellectual understanding that "the Self" wasn't an object. But because I was so used to identities, I had expected Self to feel like some super identity. As soon as I "got" that this was a major misunderstanding—and it took me two years of what I called *depression* before this happened—the ridiculousness of it hit me like a ton of bricks. Actually, it wasn't so much a "ton of bricks" as realizing that the emptiness was *so subtle.* The absence of identities is the subtlest sense. Nothing dense and heavy like "Esther."

This isn't to say I no longer had a sense of Esther, but I that I no longer experienced *being* this identity.

That's the first time you have talked about this; "I am the emptiness." When you said that something happened inside me. I'd say it made sense, but it isn't anything I can really put words to.

So for goodness sake, don't struggle to find words to it! (laughing)

You see, you want the absence of identities, but you have the habit of identities. You haven't known about anything else—other than in fleeting glimpses—since you were a tiny child. This means it is impossible for you to imagine "Self" as feeling different to an identity.

Peace and *bliss* are words that are often used to describe disidentification from the "me," but they are such connotation-filled words. The experience actually is so subtle that the best words I can think of for it are emptiness and neutrality.

My teacher Wendell wrote telling me "The disappearance of the 'me' is only known in retrospect." I just couldn't understand this, but I can tell you now, that is how it is. I was perhaps slower than most at realizing the shift in perspective. In most books it does sound as if it happens in an earth-shattering moment. That people can give a time and date and location to the *happening* surprises me.

I guess I would say the "me" began losing it's hold on my fourth day with Ramesh. But, despite the fact that seeking had been so intense, I never actually believed that in my case so-called Self-realization could happen.

I didn't actually ever think in terms of enlightenment. The word *enlightenment* was one I only associated with wizened old men in India. It never was a word that I related to. I did relate to the idea of Self-realization though, but as hard as I yearned, I never thought the yearning would end in my case.

So you say "Nothing has ever happened, and it's only a relative explanation," but you are also saying something happened.
Yes, that's the paradox. Nothing has *really* happened. Nothing has *really* changed—and everything has changed in that I no longer perceive My Self through such distorted filters. *Relatively speaking,* what happened is I stopped mistaking myself to be a concept. *In reality,* "I" have never been any concept or object, so nothing has happened to Me.

I understand that, but I just want to KNOW it! (sigh)
(laughing) You feel frustration and confusion now and it feels awful. But living life in a total fog of coping and desiring wasn't that hot either if you think about it, eh? Now, at least, you aren't

asleep to the fact that you have spent your life misconstruing Self. You now understand that you are not an object and that what you seek is not an object. Take the "frustrated seeker" and the "Sought" out of the equation and all that remains is *seeking*. Take the "seeker desiring" and "That which is desired" out of the equation and all you have left is *desiring*.

Control is recognized as an illusion, but the desire to know Your Self, minus identities, remains. As long as there is desire of any kind it means there is a sense that something is missing. If you understand that who or what You really are already Is, you understand that nothing is missing. Maybe you are thinking—as I did—"But I understand all this and still feel frustrated and more confused than ever."

That's for sure! It seems the more I understand the less I understand. It's totally confusing.
That always makes me think of the English TV comedy *Fawlty Towers*. I don't know if any of you know it, but it takes place in a horrendously mismanaged hotel. One of the staff members is this little guy called Manuel who speaks virtually no English and is a total bumbler. He's always saying, "Ai know naathink. Ai froh Barcelona!"

When *total* confusion is felt, it means the habit of thinking, "I know this," "I know that," and "This is how it is!" is being undermined. As the "me" is addicted to this way of thinking, the more confused you feel, the more it means the "me" is losing its thunder.

When there is *absolute* conviction that "Ai know naathink. Ai froh Barcelona," (laughing) that is when it becomes absolutely clear who you are NOT. First, there has to be growing confusion. I remember Ramesh saying to me that he arrived at Nisargadatta's home the first time feeling overwhelmed and totally frustrated by confusion. When I met Ramesh, that is exactly how I felt too.

When confusion is total and the desire for freedom or the desire to know Self is one-pointed, to the exclusion of ALL other desires, it means that the desire-driven, "This is how it is" oriented "me" has all but dissipated.

When *longing, desiring,* or *yearning*—for That which is beyond concepts—is all that remains, it means that the "me" has lost most of its thunder. The "me" is just a habit that cannot be sustained once you stop feeding it with thoughts of owning, becoming, controlling, and attaining.

When desire is one-pointed, to the exclusion of ALL other desires, and confusion is TOTAL, to the exclusion of any sense "I understand," there is no way the delusion of "you" can be sustained.

First there has to be the total conviction that "you" have absolutely no control. This is what gives rise to the confusion. Add to this one-pointed yearning, and there is absolutely no way the "me" delusion will continue.

If you sit in front of the guru minus any sense of "I understand something" and with nothing but total yearning to know Self, the false "you" cannot persist. In the presence of the absence of desires—which is what the Guru embodies—the final thread of desire will be broken.

If there is even one desire left, other than the desire to know Self, this can't happen.

I have been coming here so often and all I desire is Self and there is total confusion. But I still feel confused and frustrated!
This simply tells you that confusion is *not* total and desire is *not* one-pointed.

You know, when you wrote to me recently you described all kinds of phenomena and experiences that were going on with you. You asked me, "What stage of the process am I in?" You didn't ask me IF the relative process had begun; instead you simply *assumed* it had. But you wouldn't need to ask "what stage" the process is in if seeking had stopped.

Lots of people write to me, especially since my first book came out, and they give me a blow by blow description of relative processes they say they are experiencing. If I were to believe half these letters, I'd have to say "awakening" has occurred in a huge number of cases. But it's quite clear that such testimonials are very ego-based.

Ramesh and others I've read don't describe the relative process in such detail as you do.
No. And the benefit of that is perhaps that people don't latch onto those descriptions—which are only descriptions of my particular case anyway. However, it occurred to me that sincere seekers could benefit by my descriptions—although the relative process varies in each case.
Others latch onto what I've written or what I say and adopt those descriptions. So, there are pros and cons to the way I talk, but I'm only interested in the sincere seeker, so I don't care.
You see, total confusion and one-pointed yearning describes total humility. The sincere seeker shows total humility towards others and, in particular, towards the guru or teacher. When I arrived at Ramesh's home that was my experience. I took any excuse to sit as close to Ramesh's feet as possible. Although I knew he didn't like people to kiss his feet—as is the Indian custom—I totally related to that impulse. Humility was total, and the joy of it overwhelmed me.
You are still caught up in experiences. The confusion and desire may seem very strong, but until they are totally overwhelming and nothing else matters, the "me" is being sustained by the idea "it" will get something.
I'm certainly not advocating that you sit at my feet. (laughing) I'm just suggesting that humility isn't total.

But I understand that no-one "attains" enlightenment!
Then that understanding just needs to filter deeper, that's all. When it does, THEN the confusion will be total, and THEN the desire will manifest in absolute humility. If or when that happens, then there is absolutely no way the illusory "you" can continue to be mistaken for Self.
The guru embodies the absence of desires. If you sit in front of the guru and all you desire is for desiring to end, that last desire will be magnified. The pain of it, or so was my experience, is almost unbearable.

It isn't that the guru does anything. The pseudo-you is desire-based, so once it is bereft of all but this last desire "you" are on shifting sand, so to speak. In the presence of the absence of desire this final thread just snaps. But yearning or desiring has to be absolutely one-pointed. There can't be *any* other desire there.

But I can't stop buying all the new books that come out. I can't stop coming to satsang. That must mean I'm still trying to understand?
It could just be that the understanding "Ai know naathink" (laughing) is already fairly clear. If seeking is still happening, however, it's probably because you intuit that this understanding still has a ways to go. You read and come to Satsang because you intuit that these activities help the understanding to filter deeper.
If you are reading books that dispel habitual ways of thinking that's great. Unfortunately, the habit is to think selectively and to compartmentalize. You think, "I now understand that everything happens despite me." Then you go home and you wife does something you don't like and you think, "It's her fault!"

Yes, I see that happening.
The good thing is that you see that it's happening. Before you probably felt justified, and now you probably squirm because you see how selective you are in your understanding, eh?

It's just no fun anymore! (laughing)
Yes, I remember my Brazilian girlfriend coming to me and saying, *"Ah Esthehr, I used to soh enjoy getting angry with my husband and now eet ees just not de same anymore!"* (laughing)
The mind is like a set of filing drawers. In one you have filed away all your philosophical understandings: "Everything happens despite me," "Control is an illusion," etc. etc. In the other drawers you have all the old files: "I am responsible," "I create my own reality so I am guilty when something goes wrong," etc. etc. You leave here feeling that the old drawers are slowly coming under lock and key—maybe even disappearing totally. Then before you know it, they fly open and all the old programming spews out.

That's for sure! (laughing) But it does happen less and less. At least now I recognize when it is happening.
This tells you that you are no longer asleep to yourself. You no longer identify with that which once made sense and felt familiar to you. Nothing feels familiar to you anymore. How would you describe your experience now? Would you say you feel more vulnerable now you don't take such strong stances—or at least recognize it when you do?

Yes, I guess so. Well, really I just feel depressed.
But in this, what you call *depression*, there is no room for defenses is there? That's what I mean by vulnerable.

Ah, okay. Yes, I'd call that feeling very vulnerable.
To begin feeling vulnerable is to begin feeling humility. That is the first step in the unraveling. The good thing about the pain of this frustration is that it doesn't leave much time for fear or guilt. When those feelings come up, you probably can't even avoid or suppress them the way you used to, eh? Wouldn't you say it just "all hangs out" now, whereas before you found it much easier to put up fronts?

Yes, that's true.
When I reached that stage, my experience was that my "humanness" was *so glaringly human.* (laughing) Few humans ever reach a point of such vulnerability without struggling against it.
I always related to Nietzche's title *Human all too human* because I thought of my humanness as an obstacle. When I sat with Ramesh the thought that predominated in my mind was, "He's so human, he's so human!" Sitting with Ramesh—in the presence of the absence of defenses—it was the first time I really recognized that humanness was not an obstacle.
That was the greatest revelation to me. Intellectually I knew better, but the belief, "Humanness is an obstacle," had been there for so long. Ramesh embodied the *Godly* for me, yes. But it was the humanness via which It was expressed that dispelled

the belief, "Humanness is a limitation."

Perhaps now you have barely any armor or defenses left. When they come up you see them for what they are—not You. That's all that needs to happen; that gradually, the falseness of this "you" becomes glaringly obvious.

When putting up facades becomes increasingly uncomfortable—if not impossible—it means you are almost beyond the habit of coping and complacency. When you begin to see their falseness, it becomes glaringly obvious that you are separate to them and not them.

That's for sure, but they still feel painful.

Unfortunately this pain is necessary because it won't let you rest on your laurels. It keeps you awake to the illusion, seeing it more and more for what it is.

Your essential nature, or the disposition you are "born" with, is totally free of the need to cope or be complacent. You have always been free of need. Only your misperception of Self has led you to believe otherwise.

If coping and complacency are increasingly difficult for you, it means your perception of Self is losing its distortions. That you recognize the false facades when they come up—because they feel so uncomfortable and unnatural—tells you that you are much clearer on who you are NOT. It also clearly shows you, that You are separate to all those facades.

When this happens, there is just a winding down of habits. This "winding down" may not come to an end before the "death" of the body, and it may cease in the next moment. Who knows? At least, even if you feel frustrated, you aren't able to numb yourself to life anymore. The fact that more and more you are feeling *everything* fully is a huge relative change. You may not like what you feel much of the time, but isn't it better than coping and flitting from one object-desire to another—always ultimately unfulfilled?

Yes, but it's like being in no-man's-land.

Sure it is. Few people go beyond experiencing life superficially.

When you do, your "humanness" feels vulnerable and defense-less. This is why you must take advantage of this time. Savor this humanness for how you experience it now, almost void of facades and almost impossible to censor.

My experience now is of feeling more human than ever. What I called bad traits are there. What I called good traits are there. Nothing is censored, so there is the sense of feeling so incredibly ordinary, and natural, and human. Until this happened, there was always the sense of needing to be super-human, or to prove myself in some way or another—not to others really, but definitely to myself.

The idea of *perfection* is so misconstrued. The harder you aim for perfection the less likelihood there is of ever knowing it. This is because true perfection doesn't exclude anything—good or bad. Perfection describes wholeness, not a rejection or compartmentalization of anything.

The most powerful words anyone ever said to me were, "Lose interest in experiences." This was from my teacher Wendell. It took me a long time to realize just how direct these words were. I remember leaving his house and saying to John, "Those words were so important, but I don't know why."

I remember my friend Tom—whom I met while visiting Ramesh the second time—telling me that he had phoned Wayne Liquorman.—He's the author of *Acceptance of What IS, a story about nothing.* It's a great book. Tom said, "I asked him for a mantra. I knew I didn't really need one, but just thought it would help at the time. So Wayne paused for a moment and then said "fuck it'."

Probably these aren't words Wendell would ever use, but in essence Wayne was saying the same thing as Wendell. Maybe if I'd put "Lose interest in experiences" into Wayne's terms I might have understood them quicker. I still think it is the best mantra I've ever heard. (laughing)

It was only when most of the identities had *fallen away* that I began realizing, "Ah, *experiencing* is My essential nature!" It's really only then that I "got" what Wendell had meant by, "Lose interest in experiences." It's really only then that I understood why those words had had such an inexplicable impact on me. I had been so fixated on ever-changing experiences until I started asking, "How is the experiencing of anything possible?" That was when my whole orientation towards self and life began to change radically.

It can be helpful to listen to my experience of all this, and to read about those of others. In the end, no-one can learn, or rather un-learn, for you.

If words like *Grace* and *God's will* resonate deeply, and you recognize with increasing clarity that everything happens despite you, that's great. If such words perpetuate the idea that you are waiting for some-one or some-thing to *grace* "you," recognize that those concepts aren't helping you.

So are you saying Self-realization isn't by Grace, but just random? It might happen here and here and then miss me out and happen there?

I'd say *random* is a better word than *Grace* in that it doesn't have such heavy connotations. So-called *enlightenment* happens by randomness. (laughing) That's as good an explanation as any.

Self-realization is itself a term that is confusing. You will never *realize* Your Self. You only *realize* something that has been absent from an equation. You can only realize something that *hasn't* figured in an equation.

No kind of equation could even have come about if you didn't first experience being. Right now, you have too many elements in the equation, and your tally is "me-the-person, me-the-businessman, me-the mother." *Self-realization* actually signifies the realization that all these extra elements have absolutely nothing to do with the Truth of You.

This is why the seeming mystery of You is like any other mystery. As Sherlock Holmes used to say, "When you have eliminated the impossible, whatever remains, *however improbable*, must be the truth."

Emptiness seems like an improbable end to your search because you are so used to having it filled with identities. You think emptiness is an improbable end to the search so you misinterpret the increasing feeling of emptiness as *depression*. That's because there are still enough identities struggling with the experience of not feeling like *yourself*.

It's impossible to imagine being no-body, but when you begin unraveling the illusion, as improbable as it seems, you eventually conclude you can't possibly be some-body.

In one way this search is a simple process of deduction. Eliminate *you-the-seeker-object* and the *object sought* and all that remains is *seeking*. Recognize that to perceive this Seeking you have to be separate to it. And there You are, out of the picture. Of course You have never been "in the picture." The picture—the "me" identity and the whole play of manifestation—occurs only because of, and within You.

If you understand this, that's all that needs to happen. As Maharaj would say "Understanding is all." It is just a matter of this understanding filtering beyond the mind—"beyond understanding." In the meantime you may read, come to satsang, go to India, or you may wander around in frustration. You can only do whatever it is you are doing. It's just a matter of understanding that a winding down process of habitual thinking patterns will go on until it stops.

Would you ever want to give it back? I mean.....well,....
No! I think I know what you mean. No, I can't say that, but I do know that when I realized that I was no-body, there was a sense of "do I want this?" which came as a surprise.

At that point I had the experience almost of parallel worlds—there was me and there was the bodymind. This is often called the Witness stage. I spent one whole night agonizing over the thought of not having the Divine, or God, as something to direct my love towards. I understood there was no "other," but the pain of having nowhere to direct the overwhelming love and gratitude I felt was unbearable.

I think I cried for quite a few hours and just kept on repeating, "whatever it takes, what ever it takes." The next morning, the Witness sense was gone. With the disappearance of the Wit-

ness, the sense of love and gratitude towards "another" had also disappeared. Then, for a while, there was just a sense of limbo—"I am neither this nor that." Then this sense was added to. "I am neither this nor that, and I am NOT the Self!"
I was still looking for a super identity you see. I still thought Self would feel like an identity. Gradually I began to realize the subtlety of the experience and that the absence of identities doesn't reveal a "super identity" at all. You just know that you aren't any-body and that realization, of course, isn't accompanied by experiencing an identity or some-body.

So now is there just Self love?
No. Now the word *love* doesn't really make any sense to me anymore—well, not in the way it used to. I still say I love John, my husband, but actually the word doesn't make sense to me. There is just a deepening neutrality or impartiality.
Imagine someone being with you who is totally neutral; totally non-judgmental and impartial. Imagine being totally neutral with someone else.
Love really is the absence of emotions; although emotions still arise, but they subside as quickly as they come. The only way I can describe it is that they arise and subside from a place of increasing neutrality.

That would be very freeing either way.
Yes, but actually there is no sense of freedom because the sense of limitation isn't there anymore.

But I do get concerns as to how might my wife feel. She doesn't relate to any of this. But then she does seem to enjoy me more now and find me easier to live with.
Yes, you see, the idea, "If my partner isn't a seeker it will be an obstacle," is ridiculous. Or, "How will my children feel?" is another concern for lots of seekers.

Yes, I've thought about that. There does seem to be a point where a lot of questions come up—almost resistances—to going any further as it were.

209

The point is: the more one-pointed the seeking becomes, the less demanding you are of anyone else. That means you are that much more present to them as they are. How much better this is than fussing and worrying over others. It can feel like a tremendous burden when someone is constantly concerned and worrying about you, eh? And feeling worried and concerned about others is just as much of a burdensome experience.

In certain cases, a partner may find the changes daunting and they may leave. But let's face it, if that happens, your one-pointed focus will probably have eliminated the possibility of "caring" in the way you once used to anyway.

What greater gift could you offer anyone than experiencing them as they are—without judging and wanting to change them. And, the more accepting you are of your own humanness, the more you will find disconcern happening towards others. That doesn't mean you'll treat them badly. On the contrary, it means you will see them far more easily for how they are, instead of how you want or expect them to be. So it's not a matter of waiting for "everything to fall away." See the benefits that are happening already from recognizing the facades for what they are.

When you stop focusing so much on what you don't think you've "got," you'll see that what you thought you had before was cumbersome and limiting. I know it can be frustrating and painful, but this is really a time to celebrate your humanness. Recognize how uninhibited it is becoming. Even if you don't like a lot of the uncensored traits that are showing themselves, isn't it a relief to stop putting up all those fronts?

Yes.
It's what one might call the agony and the ecstasy of seeking, eh? (laughing)

Sometimes I wish I could numb off?
Ah, you do—really?

No, I guess not. No, I don't. I can't even imagine life ever having been any other way right now.

210

And that is because who you have been identified with is feeling more and more alien to you. It's like someone else's story. Once that has happened, there is no turning back. All you can do is ride it all out and enjoy the adventure for what it is— leaving behind all that is familiar.....and so limiting by its very predictability. Turning in circles, desiring this and that. How exhausting that was! (laughing)

Familiarity doesn't necessarily describe what comes naturally. After all, there are millions of men and women who stay in destructive relationships because that is all they know. That doesn't mean a familiar or common experience is healthy or natural.

Right now, you are unfamiliar with this feeling of emptiness, and you call it depression. You think it is unnatural and think of it as akin to an illness. But remember how burdensome it was having so many desires. Remember how burdensome it was accumulating and honing all those identities that used to fill the emptiness. Now, perhaps, the fleeting desires—a new boat, a new home, whatever—are falling away. Isn't there a sense of relief, of freedom that's come with this?

Yes. Yes, there is.

Right now you focus on what you think is missing from the equation—the Self—even though, intellectually, you understand that Self is merely subject to distortions. It's not missing. Eventually you just desire to stop desiring.

This is how the seeking goes. All desires have to fall away, until there remains only the one-pointed desire for liberation, or to know Self. Then the desire for this desire to go has to happen. It's the ultimate paradox, you see. (laughing) The mind in which the distortions came about is the very mechanism you use to unravel the distortions. And one-pointed desire is what brings about the falling away of all other desires.

I know as a seeker it's hard not to feel consumed by frustration. The frustration has to happen because the pain of it is what keeps you from falling back into coping and complacency. The pain of not knowing Self is something you've been a master at coping with. When this coping begins to subside, of course you're going to experience the pain of "waking up." The pain keeps you "awake" and doesn't let you fall back into the old habits.

But do recognize the up-side if you can. Enjoy this increasing sense of freedom that comes when the desires you used to have begin falling away. Finally you are beginning to experience everything more fully, rather than superficially.

Now is the time to celebrate this humanness with all its quirkiness and idiosyncrasies.

I'm trying, I'm trying! (laughing)
Unfortunately, if or when most of the identities fall by the wayside, it's really just a suicidal process—the death, as it were, of the "me." An old way of "being" is coming to an end. The familiar becomes increasingly unfamiliar, and then the unfamiliar becomes increasingly familiar.

When the "me" delusion begins to subside, it is almost always traumatic because the idea of control is still there to some degree or another.

And that's why it feels like depression?
Yes, that's why it can feel like depression, because you just don't feel like yourself anymore. The good news is that this "self" you begin to feel out of touch with is not you. This self is the veil that colors your perception of your essential, spontaneous, uninhibited nature. Because you have been familiar with the pseudo-self for so long, the falling away feels very unfamiliar. For a while you can feel as if you are in limbo, and that is what you interpret as depression.

You know, there's a fine line between clinical depression and this, what is called *spiritual emergency*. My sense is that all depressions are spiritual emergencies. On the one hand it looks like an illness and on the other hand, it has the potential of being a healing process.

If you understand these dynamics from the point of view of the dissolution of the faulty perception of self it doesn't make the experience any less traumatic to the body. This is why I feel it is still necessary to take practical steps to look after the body. A holistic approach to treatment is going to be more helpful than allopathic medicine, but you have to do what you have to do. It isn't a time to stoically disregard physical nurturing.

I want the "me" to fall away, but this fear keeps on coming up in me.
The "me" you think of as yourself is fear-based because it subsists on the desire to control. When old ways of perceiving yourself and behaving begin to subside, there is sometimes fear. It depends, I think, on how clear you are in your understanding of what is going on. But do understand, the "me" doesn't actually fall away—not in the next stage anyway. I still identify with a "me" I call Esther. It's just that now I don't think of myself as being her. The "me"—the bodymind and personality called Esther—is still apparent to me, but I know I am not her.

Were you clear on it when it was happening? I mean, did you realize what was happening—the misperception falling away?
I was clear on the dynamics of this process in terms of it happening in the case of others. But I was sure it couldn't happen in my case. This is why when certain phenomena started happening I was sure that I was going crazy. But as the process continued I struggled less and less with it. The sense just grew that, "I know nothing," and that, "There is no such thing as control." Along with that, the obsession to know Self continued to burn stronger and stronger.
There was increasing clarity in that I more and more deeply "got" that via the mind I could not find answers. Along with this, the desire for the desire to stop just grew because I realized it was the last piece holding the "me" jigsaw puzzle together. Then it was gone, and I knew with total conviction that Esther was nothing more than a delusion.

I'm so scared that the delusion might take over again and that I'll just go back to coping and give up seeking.
Ah, do you think that's possible?

*No, I guess not. No, it isn't. All I can think about is the delusion
ending.*
This kind of fear that's there now is different to the existential
fear that keeps you deluded and coping—preferring your uncomfortable comfort zone to discovering what underlies it. This
fear is what drives the sincere seeker to keep on seeking.

It sounds like it just has to be so difficult and painful.
Ah, and life was blissful and painless while you fully believed
you were the controller of your own fate? (laughing) I guess
that's why you became a seeker—because you couldn't handle
that much bliss. (laughing)
You see, you have to keep a perspective on this whole process.
You have been used to comparing yourself to others, but now is
the time to compare yourself to yourself a few years ago. Would
you want to trade your present experience in for a past experience?

*No. Even when I thought I was happy in the past, I can see fear
of the happiness stopping usually succeeded in stopping it.*
(laughing)
That's why it is important to keep a clear perspective and hone
your powers of discrimination. What would an adventure be if
it was predictable and didn't challenge you? This is the greatest
adventure you are engaged in—discovering who you are NOT.
This is why it is totally unpredictable and totally challenging.
You have the possibility of losing everything that is familiar to
you on this adventure and the funny thing is, that is exactly
what you want to happen. Are you up to the challenge? That is
the only question. You have everything at stake—everything to
lose—and in the losing of it, you will experience the ultimate
freedom.
The trouble is that all sense of limitation will be gone by then,
so you will have gained nothing. (laughing)
Right now you are still, to some degree or another, involved in
the story of "you." Gradually, as the teachings filter deeper, this
story will seem more and more surreal. That is, the altered state
of being hypnotized by this "me" idea will show itself to be an

altered state. The more deeply this is felt the harder you will try to wake up, and the more intense the seeking will become.

It sounds like being stoned, having a bad trip, and just wanting it to end. (laughing)
Yup, that's a pretty good analogy. (laughing) Like a bad trip, you have absolutely no idea when or how this delusion will wear off and there isn't a damn thing "you" can do that will cause it to wear off. The harder you try, the more deeply you understand that it is all totally out of your hands.

If all that's left is the desire for desiring to stop, then it can't not happen—the end of the delusion I mean? Is that what you said earlier?

The delusion of "you" is held together, so to speak, by mutually perpetuating desires. When all but the desire to stop desiring remains there is almost nothing left to keep the delusion going. Then it's just a matter of time and whether or not the body "dies" beforehand.

Thank you.

Before seeking begins you are like someone who is having a bad drug trip but has forgotten that he is on drugs and thinks what he is seeing is real. When you begin to understand that YOU are not an object you are like someone who is having a bad drug trip but knows that he is hallucinating.

In the same way you cannot make the effects of a drug wear off, you cannot make the hallucination "I am some-body" wear off. The first step is to know that who you think you are is an illusion. Once you deeply understand this, the delusion has already begun to wear off. There is nothing you can do to accelerate this process. "Understanding is all."

Self-Realization - the Paradox

I've heard it said that the jnani, can be a madman, a drunkard, a fool. Can you explain that?
"Awakening" can happen via any bodymind. There are usually certain factors that seem to coincide with "awakening" but it can happen via any bodymind.

But it's hard to imagine that there can be addictions such as alcoholism after awakening?
If at the time of "awakening" there are chemical imbalances, they may stop and they may continue.

But I thought addictions only happened when an emotion or a memory was being suppressed. Addiction means dependency. Why would the jnani experience dependency or be suppressing anything?
Ah, a *reason* for addictions! (laughing)
From a psychoanalytical standpoint, it appears that the suppression of emotional trauma can lead to addictions and dependency. From a psychoanalytical and medical standpoint, there are millions of *possible* reasons for addiction and/or mental imbalance. No-one has been able to pinpoint an absolute reason for these imbalances. If prior to awakening addiction or mental imbalance was happening, it won't necessarily cease. If these ailments were already in potential in the body, they may even surface after awakening.

But how is that possible? Once the emotional holdings are gone, and guilt and fear are gone, why would addictions happen? That sounds like neediness, and surely neediness is gone too?
While there is a physical body through which awakening hap-

pens, that body is still subject to imbalances. Certain jnani's have amazing powers, or *sidhis* (magic tricks) and can drink and take drugs with no side affects. Others have no such powers.

There are certain martial artists that have built up the Wei Qi, or protective energy of their bodies—who aren't awakened as such—and their bodies can undergo incredible hardship and they experience no detrimental affects.

You see, all bodies are different. So depending on the particular body, whatever happens just happens.

Addiction does signify need, but from the jnani's point of view, the need or addiction doesn't reflect on him as a person. He doesn't think any the worse of himself because there's an addiction. If the *ajnani* experiences addiction, it's very different. He sees the lack of control as a reflection of his own weakness as a person. He sees addiction as a personal stigma that means he's "lesser than," or "weaker than."

Doesn't the jnani still struggle with it though?
Let's say that the jnani has a very bad injury and is put on pain-killers. If addiction is in potential in his body, he may become dependent on the painkillers. In order to come off them, if that is the decision, he'll probably have to undergo withdrawals in the same way you would.

Then would that experience be underlain by peace? Would that be the difference?
When I say all experiences are underlain by peace, it means that all experiences are felt fully. It's only the effort to avoid experiencing that keeps you out of touch with your essentially peaceful nature.

If the experience is of struggling with symptoms of withdrawal, this experience would be fully felt. Peace might not be felt as overtly as it is when such a struggle isn't happening, but in comparison to the ajnani there would be a centeredness within the struggle.

That's really hard to understand. Struggle and centeredness sounds like a contradiction in terms.

Yes, it is a contradiction in terms, and a word for *contradiction in terms* is paradox.

I know it is very hard for you to understand that peace and struggle can be experienced simultaneously, but when struggle is experienced *fully*, that is the case.

When struggle isn't considered personal, and the potential outcome isn't considered a measure of personal strength or weakness, there's a very different perspective.

The peace might only be experienced subtly at that point. It all depends at what stage of the relative process this happens.

Can you talk about that process a bit?
I can talk about my experience of it. It may be different in other cases.

You know I make a differentiation between identifying *as* and identifying *with*. The ajnani thinks of himself as being the bodymind. The jnani knows he has a bodymind that is unique to him, and he is identified *with* it, but he knows he isn't it. He has a unique personality—what we call the "I"—but he knows he isn't this unique expression.

*It seems like such a subtle difference between identifying **as** and identifying **with**. I know it's not subtle, but at the same time....*
It's almost like a flick of a switch that cessation of identifying *as* to identifying *with*. At first it can be so subtle that it is easy to miss. Something has changed, but you can't quite put your finger on it. At least that was my experience. It seems to be different in all cases. Retrospectively, I guess I would pinpoint the *throwing of the switch* when I first sat in front of Ramesh. But it was only very retrospectively that I could say that.

But the ones I've read of all sounded as if they knew instantly.
Yes, I had that impression too. All I know is that my experience was different. There were many habits that needed to fall away. For a start, I was so convinced it could never *happen* in my case that it didn't matter what anyone told me about their observations of me, I didn't believe them. Now I have a better under-

standing of why that was.

I really didn't "get" the concept of identification *with* being there afterwards.

I know John and others I've talked to often thought about what it might feel like if awakening *happened*. I never even considered what it might be like because I was sure it wouldn't happen.

But if you wanted it so much, how could you not have at least hoped it would happen?
It's strange perhaps, but the yearning was so all-consuming that I didn't think about outcome.

How can you yearn that hard and not think about outcome?
What was, the ignorance of Self, frustrated me so much. It was the frustration of the yearning that took all my focus. After all, frustration and yearning aren't that different really.

I deeply understood that what I yearned for wasn't missing, so my focus wasn't towards a goal in the usual sense. I just wanted the misperception to stop. Maybe that constitutes the same as aiming for Self, but all I could really think about was the misperception ending. That seemed so highly improbable—impossible even—that there just seemed to be me and endless searching.

Perhaps I hoped, but I think my conviction that it couldn't happen in my case pretty much cancelled hope out. In a way I felt relieved to feel such strong yearning because all other yearnings had stopped. I guess it's rather like someone who finds themselves in a terrible situation that, in and of itself affords them a vocation. Yearning just felt like the vocation I'd never found. I know it sounds weird, but that's how I recall it. It isn't that there was resignation there—"I'll keep on searching, but know I'll never awaken." The search was undertaken so fully and so one-pointedly that there was just the search.

So once it happened and you understood it had, what was the process then?
At first I came to the conclusion, "experiencing is all there is." I thought, "Ah, that's what Ramesh meant by, "Consciousness is

all there is."

For about a year I think, there were strong phenomena happening in my body. Habits of interaction that had become increasingly dynamic from the onset of interaction with the world began falling away, changing. As a result, my sense of relationships changed dramatically. There was an increasing neutrality towards others, especially those very close to me.

During that time there were no more questions. There was just a deepening sense of peace. When that stabilized quite strongly, suddenly questions started arising again.

I thought there were no more questions afterwards.
That had been my impression too, and maybe in some cases there aren't any more questions. In my case, questions started bubbling up all over again.

I knew I wasn't any concept and all that was left was experiencing. Then I thought, "But experiencing ends with the 'death' of the body" so clearly I'm not this consciousness.

So you understood you weren't the personality?
It was totally clear to me that this expression of Consciousness happening through my body, and that happening through other bodies, is all the same Consciousness. And I understood, or the knowing is there, that I am the impersonal functioning of Consciousness happening in Totality. The knowing also is that consciousness ends when the body "dies," and that Consciousness and the Absolute are not-two.

The thoughts and questions that started coming were as follows. The knowing is that Consciousness plus the Absolute are not-two. That my manifest nature and my non-manifest nature are not-two. I deeply understand paradox for what it is—two sides of the same coin. The paradox is that as long as my essential, paradoxical nature is the orientation, this knowing is from the perspective of one side of the coin, so to speak.

Can you explain that?
Yes. You see, I know that I am not the bodymind or the "I"—

personality, but I still identify *with* them. The knowing of who I am not is happening via the mechanism of the bodymind, and I am identified with it.

I know that I am the impersonal functioning happening in Totality, but because this knowing is happening via a personal bodymind and a unique "I," it can't be said that functioning is experienced as *absolutely* impersonal.

But if you know you aren't a body or any object, how can anything be personal?

Clearly nothing is personal. Even the words *"my* body," which denote ownership, aren't related to as before because I know there's no such thing as "mine." However, as long as I am identified *with*—albeit no longer *as*—this bodymind, the knowing is still somewhat subjective.

What do you mean by subjective?

While you think you are an object, your perspective is totally subjective. It isn't objective at all. You think you are an object who owns and experiences an object. That's very subjective thinking.

I know I'm not the body or any other concept, so one could say thinking is more objective now. Relatively speaking, in comparison to ajnani—ignorance of Self—it *appears* as if thinking is totally objective. This is because there isn't the involvement there was before. But because the wordless knowing is happening via my unique intellect and via my unique bodymind, this constitutes a relationship or a form of involvement.

Clearly this kind of *involvement* bears little or no resemblance to what was happening while I thought I was the body. The paradox is that as long as the understanding that actions are impersonal is happening through a personalized body, that constitutes a relationship, and an involvement of sorts. This means that thinking is not absolutely objective. It is a variation on subjective thinking only. Perhaps a big variation, relatively speaking, but it's still only a variation.

Because the knowing that I am not any concept is happening in

relation to a concept—the bodymind—one can only call this knowing a *deep intuiting*. One can't call it absolute Knowledge.

I'm a bit lost.
I know my essential, manifest nature, and my non-manifest nature are not-two. I know they are two sides of the same coin.
But, as long as my essential nature—knowing—is the orientation,
this knowing is from the perspective of one side of the coin only.

*You know you talk about the veil of ignorance? Well now it sounds
as if one veil has dropped only to find another.*
You know "I am," and right now that knowing is somewhat distorted because you have added, "I am this and that" to the equation of You. I know "I am," and there is no longer any distortion
in this knowing. The similarity between us is that in both cases
there is *knowing*. That knowing, whatever it looks like, is still
knowing and that is Your essential nature. So the veil isn't anything other than your essential nature.
The first step in the relative process is for distorted perception to
stop. You have to realize that Your essential nature isn't hidden
from you. You know that you are, and that knowing is Your essential nature. You experience being, and that is Your essential
nature.
Just because you experience being a body, it hasn't changed Your
essential nature in any way. That is the first step, understanding
that who You are already is, and that this has never been hidden
from you.
That's what is meant by, "The seeker is the Sought." Actually it
might be clearer to say the *seeking* is the Sought. And when
seeking stops, whatever other function is happening is the Sought.
Your essential nature is Experiencing or Consciousness.

*I thought once that was really understood and awakening hap-
pened—you know what I mean—that that was all there was to it.*
That was exactly what I thought too, and for a while I thought
that was it. I just thought there would be an ongoing process of
the peace deepening. I certainly didn't expect any questions at all.

Then I started wandering around saying to myself, "But this isn't 'it'!" "This isn't all there is to it." It suddenly became clear to me that as long as the knowing was happening via a bodymind and there was identification *with* it, the impersonality of actions was still only a deep intuiting. As long as this knowing was centered around "Esther" or this unique personality—we'll call it the "I"— as long as knowing was centered around the "I," it was, to a degree, colored by that "I."

But if you know you aren't it, why does that matter?
It doesn't "matter" in the sense that I don't worry about it. There isn't the frustration that was there when I was seeking, as such. My experience now is of a deepening dispassion or a deepening neutrality towards everything, including this "I." As this dispassion deepens, it's as if there is a deepening Self-absorption. Orientation is turning away from this "I" and the mind is increasingly "absorbed" by the sense of peace.

Can you explain a bit more?
The best way I can describe it is that what once felt familiar suddenly feels totally unfamiliar, and then the "unfamiliar" suddenly feels totally familiar. I can't even relate to having felt any other way before.
I see this happening in the way I relate to others, particularly in my close relationships, such as with John, my husband. For a while it will feel as if everything familiar about our relationship has gone and everything feels totally unfamiliar. Then it all feels so natural and I can't define what change might have happened. Of course, defining the change is impossible because the change is the falling away of something that defined our relationship.

But you still feel like you're married to him?
Neither of us relate to marriage in the usual sense, but less now than ever.
There was never a strong neediness in our marriage, and we never put strong expectations on each other. We were in the relationship from the start to better know ourselves. We weren't

in it out of a fear of being alone, or with the expectation of our relationship developing a certain way. I think we both were very conscious from the beginning that we were about un-defining ourselves together, rather than re-defining ourselves together. Now, for both of us, any definitions that came about—as they almost always do in any relationship—any such definitions are falling away.

As the familiar becomes unfamiliar and then the "unfamiliar" familiar, there is a stabilizing that happens. So you see, this process, the way I see it, is about degrees of involvement still falling away. Other words for *involvement* might be habits of interaction. It means that our relationship is more flowing than ever, less restrictive than it once was—although by average standards, I don't think either of us ever experienced the other as any kind of limitation. What I did experience early on was that being in a committed relationship helped me see the restrictions I had been placing on myself because of expectations.

So now there aren't any expectations?
There are still some habits there because I have come to know John's habits. In getting to know his habits, my habits adapted accordingly. Now both of us experience a falling away of habits, both in ourselves and in each other. That's why sometimes there are periods when we can't pinpoint a change, but it's clear something has happened.

I guess the feeling during this process has been that whatever "joined" us is disappearing.
Maybe you can understand it this way. You have a unique personality and so does your husband. You come together and your personalities clash and complement each other. This combination of clashing and combining and how it sums itself up is what usually makes up a relationship.

You are born with unique traits and characteristics that make up your personality, as is the case for everybody. With the onset of interaction, these characteristics start being defined in more and more dynamic ways. While you mistake yourself to be somebody, these definitions to your personality are very strong. When you realize who you are not, these definitions start losing definition, so to speak.

In John's and my case, in different ways, this process of losing definition is happening. This means that the clashing and complementing that was previously happening between us is changing dramatically. As each of our personalities is losing definition, our relationship is losing definition. There is still a relationship between two unique personalities and two unique bodies, but it is very different.

I don't know if I can ask this, but do you still have sex? If there is dispassion or neutrality, does that mean disinterest?

If I give you details about our personal relationship that isn't of any use to you. Each case is very different, so having specific expectations about this is of no use.

What I'm trying to communicate is that relationships—be they with loved ones or people in general—undergo change as the "I" undergoes change. One could say there is disinterest, but it isn't in the form of rejection as you think of it.

The whole idea of rejecting or accepting isn't really a part of this. There is just a falling away of the habit of involvement. Because involvement is about strong feelings and strong actions, dispassion is really about a mellowing of all that. Emotions are actually stronger than ever before, when they surface. What is different is that they happen at the most unexpected times and not necessarily where one would expect them to surface.

That's because in the ajnani stage habits exist even around when and where you do and don't let emotions surface. Now emotions come and go, and because they are felt and expressed fully, they aren't really of any concern.

So dispassion is really a deepening of disconcern rather than a deepening of disinterest. I guess it's all just words, but *disinterest* has a strong reactionary connotation to me. Dispassion isn't reactionary at all. On the contrary, it's the diluting of reactionary behavior.

As this process of deepening dispassion continues it's as if I am absorbing the story of Esther back into My Self. Another way of saying this is that it's as if identification *with* is losing its strength.

You mean you feel like you don't have a body?
This process is so subtle, except during the periods when every-thing feels unfamiliar, that it's hard to explain. I still feel like I have a body. I am not oblivious of my body. It's just that my focus towards my body is changing.
There are habits we all have towards our bodies. The way we take care of it and the way we make it look. Those habits are very strong. Some of them are nurturing and necessary second nature functions, but the majority of them are really unimportant. Those latter kinds of habits are all falling away—some of them gradually, some of them quickly.

So what are the questions you have now?
Well, it's clear to me that I only experience one side of the coin of My Self. That is, I know my essential, manifest nature for what it is, but my non-manifest nature is only intuited. I know that when the body "dies," consciousness will cease animating it. I know that this consciousness isn't the sum total of Me.
I know that I am the impersonal functioning of Consciousness in Totality; that the Consciousness expressing through your body is the exact same Consciousness as is expressing it-Self through mine. I only know about this because I experience being. When the body "dies," this experience will end. As this experience, this "I," ends with the death of the body, it isn't real. It is only a tempo-rary appearance, so I know I can't BE it.

But Consciousness is the Self, so you are it surely?
Self-consciousness is a reverse reflection of the Absolute unaware of it-Self, or the un-Self-conscious Absolute. In this way, yes, my essential nature *is* an aspect of Me, but this aspect or appearance is temporary, and the words *temporary* and *relative* mean non-absolute.
Via this reverse reflection of the Absolute—which is My Self—I know that "I am." Initially, "I am this and that" is the faulty perception that happens. When this misperception clears up I know about myself in clearer terms. I know about My reflec-

227

tion—this manifest appearance—and, seeing it clearly, I enjoy it more than ever. I enjoy Being more than ever.
Gradually—my experience of the process is—this enjoyment or love of being begins to change. There is less and less physical tension, and less and less emotional tension. Peace deepens, and everything is experienced more fully.
Gradually, habits of interaction fall away and there is a deepening disconcern, even for this Beingness.

But that sounds almost as if you must feel like you're dying?
Yes. That is exactly how it feels. Between the ajnani and the jnani stage, this "feeling like you're dying" is often interpreted as depression. The primary identities—gender, age, name, roles, etc.—cease being identified *as*. It's a very traumatic experience.
To me now, this ongoing process is like a variation on, or replay of the ajnani to jnani stage. The difference is that now there isn't the existential fear that tinged the first stage of the process. Minus that fear, there isn't depression. But at times there have been sudden moments when the thought came again, "I feel like I'm dying," and even strong grief. But it has been very temporary and then it was gone. Then there was a sense of disorientation for a while, and that passes and I felt more natural, more "normal" than ever.

But the questions?....
It is clear to me that identification *with* is changing. I am still identified *with* labels, the body and the mind—not AS them—but there is something different about this experience, and it's constantly changing.
As a result of this experience, it's clear to me that while the body is around, it is possible that identification *with* ceases totally, or disappears to but a trace. At least this is my sense of what can happen in certain cases.
When I fall into deep, dreamless sleep and then wake up, like you, retrospectively I know that I was unaware of myself. This is why the realm of manifestation is also called the realm of knowing and not-knowing.

I know that my True nature is beyond the manifest, beyond knowing and not-knowing. I understand the dynamics of paradox, and My Self in terms of paradox. The big paradox is that I know I am not a bodymind, but I am still identified *with* it; I am still oriented in relation to it. I intuit the whole coin—Absolute plus consciousness are not-two—but while this knowing is happening in relation to the particular aspect of duality called "Esther" there isn't total objectivity on this.

Whether there is identification AS, or identification WITH, one must call this perspective a subjective one. That is, a relationship of any kind denotes an involvement and where there is involvement there cannot be absolute objectivity.

While the Subject or Absolute is only known via the intermediary reflection of the bodymind that *knowing* is subjective.

Can you repeat that?
When the realization happens that you are not the bodymind and not *any* object it is quite clear that everything you perceive is unfolding within You. However, because this sense is centered around the bodymind, it is still only quasi-objective.

Why is it clear that everything is happening within you?
As You aren't an object, it means You are dimensionless, infinite. As You are infinite, clearly objects, appearances, must be appearing *within* You. It can't be the other way around. What comes first something or nothing?

Nothing.
Yes, something cannot precede nothing. Another way of saying this is that you can't have an object before you have a non-object. As objects come and go, you can't say they have any absolute existence unto themselves. Nothingness doesn't come and go, which means it exists.

You mean the absence of existence exists!?
If something is true today and not tomorrow, you can't say it was ever a truth. Similarly, if something "exists" today and not tomor-

row, you can't say it ever had any real existence. It "existed" relatively speaking, and the word *relative* has its roots in the definition *non-absolute.* If something isn't absolute it isn't real. It seems to be temporarily real, but that doesn't describe reality does it? Reality, existence, is something you have absolutely no doubt about, and you can only be minus doubts about the existence of something if it exists permanently.

What do you mean? I'm confused.
If you see a chair here now, then look away, and then look back and it's gone, can you be sure it was ever there?

No, I guess not.
Something that comes and goes isn't something you can be sure about. You can't say something exists for sure unless you know without a doubt that it will always exist. People talk about the end of the world. They don't know it will happen, but the fact that they talk about the end of the world means that they intuit that the world had a beginning. If the world, manifestation, had a beginning, then what came before it?

Nothing.
Nothing is the only conceptual solution you can come up with. But you know "I am"; you experience being, and think, "I exist." How do you know this? How is it possible that you know you exist? Where did this knowing come from?

From not-knowing?
But who or what was *not-knowing*? You have to know, "I am" before you can know that you were in deep sleep, unaware of yourself. What happens to the world and to your body when you are in deep sleep? Are you sure they don't just disappear and reappear when you wake up?

No. I don't know that.
This tells you that there has to be Awareness before anything can be known. Before your birth you didn't know about yourself.

Does that mean you didn't exist? Are you sure that prior to your "birth" you didn't exist? Can you know that for sure? Do you know for sure that when you wake up after dreamless sleep that isn't your first day of life?

I have a history, a past.
But the past is past, not here now. Is it any different to a chair that you see and then don't see. How can you be sure the past is real? You have a family, memories, friends, roles, but who's to say all that and the "memory" of it, hasn't all appeared in the moment you wake up?

I can't be sure.
The only clue you have to Your Self is this experience of being, this "I am" sense you have. It began with the "birth" of the body and ends with its "death." Before "birth" you didn't know about yourself. After "birth" you know "I am."
If you don't know about yourself and then know about yourself, doesn't that tell you that YOU have to have existed all along?
If you are unaware of something, and then aware of something, what is the common denominator in this equation.

Awareness or lack of awareness.
Can awareness be created out of the absence of awareness?

No. Ah, so there has to be awareness, it's just unaware of itself.
So these are the only concepts we can come up with—awareness and nothingness.
Who you are prior to consciousness, prior to Self-awareness, might be called awareness and it might be called no-thingness. Neither concept gives you a solution to the existence of You does it?

No. It's just concepts and we aren't any concept.
Exactly. You are prior to concepts, which means you are prior to consciousness or "I amness" because they are concepts you know about. You have to be prior to this knowing and prior to the not-knowing you know about when you wake up from deep sleep.

First you have to know, with total conviction, that you are not a concept. This conviction isn't an intellectual one because the mind and intellect can only conceptualize. They can't conceive of a non-concept. So in the jnani stage, the *knowing* is, "I am not a concept." The paradox of this knowing is that it happens via the mechanism of the conceptualizing mind.

So you know you're not a concept because of a concept, is that what you're saying? (laughing)
The body doesn't *cause* you to experience being. Do be clear on that. However, this experience is dependant on there being a body.
You know about Your non-objective Self via an object, yes.
When the realization happens that You are not this object the bodymind doesn't cease to be experienced. You just know You are NOT it or any other concept and yo know this via the mechanism of the body.
The knowing "I am" is happening in millions of bodies. The way Consciousness expresses it-Self through one body is very different to how it expresses it-Self through another but it is all the same Consciousness.
It is clear to me that "I am-consciousness" is not fragmented because it has taken on various modes of expression. However, while I am still identified *with* Esther, albeit not *as* her, I still experience relative differences in Self-expression.

But you know these differences aren't real?
Yes, I know there is no real difference. However, as long as there is identification *with* one particular aspect of duality, my non-dual nature still has a dualistic appearance.

But if you know it's not real that makes a huge difference, doesn't it?
Yes, that is a huge shift in perspective compared to before. That is only the first step though. First you have to be quite clear that You are not an appearance. Once you know, without a shadow of a doubt that You are not any-thing, perspective is much more

objective. Until you cease identifying with the "I," however, your perspective is still only quasi-objective.

Well, I'd be happy if I just had quasi-objectivity! (laughing)
The shift in perspective is day and night compared to how you experienced yourself beforehand. However, this isn't the end of the process. You have to stay quite clear on this because if you don't the process probably won't unravel fully.

Shankara pointed to this when he said, "Even though you may have reached a stage at which the universe and its creatures appeara as dream-images only....you must still strive ceaselessly to destroy the illusion."

By "striving" he didn't, of course, refer to personal effort. He was basically pointing out that the process is incomplete and that you have to keep perspective. You have to realize that your perspective is still only quasi-objective.

Only when the "I" subsides does perspective become absolutely objective.

I don't quite get it.
Until identification with the illusory "you" ceases the knowing of Your non-dual nature is deeply intuited via one particular aspect of duality. When this aspect or "I" subsides Self is no longer an indirect knowing happening from the standpoint of a dream-image called "me" or "I."

But you know you aren't that dream-image!
It's like this. Let's say you go to bed and dream. For a while you think you are the person in the dream but then, within the dream, you realize you are dreaming. That's what is often called lucid dreaming.

The dream continues and you continue to experience playing a role in the dream, all the while knowing that this role is nothing real.

In my opinion the jnani stage is similar to lucid dreaming. The jnani knows that manifestation is only a bunch of dream-images and that he is not the dream-figure around which this knowing is centered. There are no doubts about this so one could say that the jnani is way more "lucid" than before. That manifestation is only a dream, an illusion, is clear but until the jnani no longer figures in the dream one can't say *he* is fully "awake."

That sounds like the Twilight Zone? (laughing)
Yes, I guess that's one way of putting it. It's like the stage between dreaming and waking up. There is lucidity but you are not fully awake.
In the morning when you wake up fully you know it was just a dream. The difference is that the waking and dreaming states of daily life are really both variations on dreaming.
The jnani must keep a clear perspective on all this until the dream-image of "him" ceases totally. That is when the dream is witnessed from beyond the dream, so to speak. As long as the body-mind continues there will be a perception of it, but it won't take center stage anymore.
You the Absolute are then center stage. Or perhaps one could say it would be more like being right in the back of the audience, just watching everything unfold.
From this perspective "I am" is whole. It is no longer merely intuited as being whole.

Can you explain that some more?
Right now I know that "I am" or Consciousness has no boundaries. I know it is the same "I am" happening through all bodies. However, the expression of "I am" happening through the body called "Esther" is central to this knowing. As long as one particular dream-figure or bodymind is central to "I am," it seems as if "I am" is more strongly defined where that bodymind is concerned. When the "I" subsides it means that bodymind is no longer central to the experience "I am." The dream is no longer witnessed from the standpoint of the body-object but from the standpoint of the Absolute or Subject.
When this *happens*, the wholeness of "I am" is fully known. There is total or absolute objectivity rather than quasi-objectivity. And don't get me wrong. What I call "quasi-objectivity" is not

something to scoff at. Relatively speaking, it is a quantum shift in perspective.

But you are much more objective than before.
There can't be degrees of objectivity in the same way there can't be degrees of control, or degrees of truth. Either there is absolute objectivity, absolute control, and absolute truth or there isn't any. Relatively speaking there appears to be more objectivity, but this is just a relative perception. And *relative* means non-absolute or partial.
In jnani, one could say there is more objectivity. The whole coin of paradox (that Absolute and "I am-consciousness" are not-two) is deeply intuited, but absolute objectivity is not the experience.
There can only be absolute objectivity when the "I" is out of the picture. The intermediary to knowing about Your Self is "I-consciousness," or experiencing. Who you really are precedes this consciousness. You are the Subject within which this object-appearance has arisen. You the Subject have assumed this object-appearance.

I get muddled. Can you explain the difference between subject and object?
Before there can be a reflection in a mirror, a subject has to stand in front of the mirror. Before a portrait can be painted, there has to be a subject to paint. Before Your manifest objective appearance came about, there had to be a Subject to be reflected.
I know that I am not the objects I experience—which includes this "I" or personality—and I know that I precede all objects. I know that because I experience objects they have to be present within Me. It's not the other way around. I know that the body doesn't contain Me, but that it, and all of manifestation, is My content.
Because I experience knowing this via an object, one can only say that this knowing is a deep intuiting.

Does it matter though? I mean, now who you thought you were is out of the picture.

Who I thought I was isn't actually out of the picture. I, who I really am, is out of the picture, but I only experience this because the picture or story of Esther is still identified *with*—albeit not *as*. I am out of the picture, but identification WITH a particular object in the picture stops me from seeing the picture as a whole. Identification WITH this particular bodymind inhibits direct, objective knowledge of the picture as a whole.

The knowing or intuiting is that I am apart from the picture, in that *it* isn't Reality. However, I only know about my Real nature via a relative concept. That is the paradox, and who or what I really am is prior to paradox, prior to duality.

I know I am not just the head of the coin, or the tail of the coin, so to speak. I know I am the whole coin—the Absolute plus Consciousness as not-two. But I only know this from the perspective of one side of the coin, and we can call that *side* "Esther."

My concept is that there is a pulsation within the Absolute, an arising and subsiding, and we call that Consciousness. With each arising and subsiding of the Absolute, universes are created and destroyed. With the appearance of each bodymind, one could say a droplet of Consciousness is superimposed upon, or assumes a manifest appearance. Each droplet is unique in its own way, but all the droplets are still only Consciousness.

The droplet plus the bodymind give rise to "I am." The uniqueness of this appearance gains definition, and "I am" is misconceived to be "I am this and that." The reversal of this process begins when the "this and that" falls away. The belief "I am somebody," subsides and what remains is, "I am nobody," but this knowing still happens via a body that is *personal* or unique to that particular droplet of consciousness. That's the paradox.

The droplets of consciousness are all the same, but each unique body type and its characteristics give those droplets of consciousness relative definition.

When the knowing happens that all the droplets are the same Consciousness, that is the first stage of the reversal process. The next stage is when you cease identifying *with* the unique expression of Consciousness happening through a particular body; what we call "I."

But then you'd be totally disoriented and lost surely?
If you are not an object but think you are, I'd say that describes disorientation and being lost. (laughing) If you know there is no real difference between you and anyone else, but still experience differences, that still denotes disorientation to me.
I know I am not this consciousness that will end with the "death" of the body. I know I'm not this droplet and it's superimposed "I." But I still experience this knowing from the perspective of the "I," and that describes *disorientation* to me.
So the ongoing process is a re-orienting away from this "I." During this process there are times when there can be strong feelings of disorientation until these "shifts" are adapted to. For example, I sometimes experience intense dizziness during these times. As John likes to say: "Before enlightenment, dizzy blonde. After enlightenment, dizzy blonde!" (laughing)
When the "I" subsides, "others" would still experience a personality, albeit minus so many learned habits. From the perspective of the Sat-guru the strong sense of being related to a particular bodymind would have ceased. The body would still be evident, but the Sat-guru's sense of it would be similar to the relationship you have with your shadow. There wouldn't be any strong involvement with the body anymore.
Although now I know there is no in and out of who I am, to a degree I still experience in and out because the body is identified with. When that identification totally subsides, IF it does while the body is "alive," this experience would cease. There would be no sense of in and out. The "wholeness" of Self would then be experienced directly rather than indirectly intuited.
The jnani experiences emotions fully, rather than superficially. This is why he experiences life in a much more peaceful way. The desire to maintain or resist emotions is totally gone. However, even though he knows that no situation can have any affect on *him*, diverse emotions are still the experienced in relation to whatever is happening.
In Sat-guru there is only the feintest thread, so to speak, linking focus to the body. This is why Sat-guru is the embodiment of

absolute peace.

The jnani is increasingly Self-absorbed. And I don't mean this in the usual sense. As dispassion or disconcern for manifestation deepens so does the sense of peace. The mind is increasingly absorbed by or into this peace. However, while the mind still has the tendancy to re-orient towards whatever is going on in the world, the sense of peace can vascillate. It certainly increases and stabilizes as habits of interaction fall away, but peace isn't total. Although there are no strong needs where interaction is concerned, the mind still boots up commentaries on what is going on. This is very different to the strong judgments that were there before, but any form of judgment still constitutes a form of involvement.

In Sat-guru the dream is over. Then there is total Self-absorption or absorption in Reality. There is absolute peace and when interaction needs to happen, it happens from the standpoint of this peace. There is absolutely no involvement, no judgment, no prejudice.

It's so hard to imagine. I feel so angry now. It seemed simple until today, and now I just feel like I'm back to square one.

And that is part of this whole reversal process. You think you know something, and in following this type of thinking to its extreme you realize more and more deeply you know absolutely nothing. And the paradox is that even the understanding, "I know nothing," supposes knowledge of something.

In this way the paradoxical seems more and more paradoxical by the moment. And the understanding "I know nothing" is one you keep on coming back to.

My experience is this; that the circular nature of mind is more and more evident. As the knowing, "I know nothing," deepens, the mind *departs* from, and *returns* to, the same point constantly.

It's not that I sit around thinking in these terms all the time, but because the questions have arisen and these trains of thought have been followed, the circles spin ever-tighter. This is the ongoing process, words subsiding into themselves, the mind spiraling in on itself. And this is how it goes until there is but an almost still point where "I know nothing" is all that remains. My sense is that in that moment this paradoxical thought subsides within itself. That is what is meant by *transcending the mind* or transcendental Consciousness. No-one transcends any-thing, of course, but the intermediary of intellect subsides from the equation.

That sounds like how you described seeking. That you have to get to a point where you know you can't understand anything with the mind.

Exactly, yes. Do you see, the process from ajnani to jnani works like that? Then the ongoing relative process from jnani to Sat-Guru is a variation on the same theme. As a seeker you experience frustration. I don't experience frustration, but I experience dispassion, disconcern. Dispassion is just the other side of the coin of frustration—concern. Until experiencing ceases happening from the perspective of one side of the coin only, the whole coin is only intuited.

When the "I" subsides there is absolutely objective, absolutely impersonal Knowledge of all this. The whole process reverses itself, and when this happens during the "life" of the body, the "one" via which this happens is the embodiment of absolute Knowledge.

One could say they are the embodiment of the non-dual "within" duality. This embodiment is often referred to as *Sat-guru*. In my opinion only the Sat-guru embodies full enlightenment.

And remember, *enlightenment* is just a description of a relative concept. It is the description of a relative difference. *Full enlightenment* describes the difference between ajnani (one ignorant of Self) and Sat-guru (the embodiment of absolutely impersonal Knowledge).

One can make a relative distinction between what the jnani embodies as compared to the ajnani. The jnani, in my opinion, can be considered to be the embodiment of a degree of enlightenment, but as far as I'm concerned, *a degree* of enlightenment doesn't constitute enlightenment. Lucid dreaming doesn't constitute being "awake."

This, of course, is my perspective now. It is the perspective from the standpoint of jnana or knowing. From the standpoint of ajnana or ignorance of Self, sitting in the presence of that degree of enlightenment can have very strong impact. That is because there is a huge relative difference and, in the case of the sincere open-minded seeker, that relative difference is strongly felt. If you deeply understand that you are ignorant of Your Self, when you are in the presence of the jnani the relative difference may be felt very strongly.

What do you mean by "the relative difference" exactly?
When I sat with Ramesh and with Wendell I was painfully aware of an armoring over my heart. To me, both Ramesh and Wendell felt transparent. The experience of their transparency seemed to highlight my "armoring." It was the first time that I felt what I would call the *covering* of ignorance. Once that had been high-lighted it wasn't something I could ever be oblivious to again. The pain of it became more and more intense during the first days I was with Ramesh. It was as if the "armor" over my heart was trying to break. Then on the fourth day it was gone.

Listening to you speak it just seems like paradox upon paradox!
Yes, or like paradox within paradox within paradox. That's what I mean by the mind spiraling in upon itself. As paradox is more and more deeply experienced, it throws the mind in upon itself. And the great paradox is that although I know the mind is inca-pable of understanding Me, the paradox is that the mind still aims for the most extreme imagery and understanding possible. That's why, to me, this stage of the process is like a variation on the ajnani (ignorance of Self) to jnani stage (Self knowing). The dif-ference is that perspective is far clearer. In the ajnani stage the mind reached a point where the futility of trying to understand was fully recognized.

So why are questions pursued in this stage? If in the jnani stage it is totally clear that nothing can be understood, why do questions start all over again?
Now there isn't a striving in the sense of personal efforts.

It's clear to me that no answers have any bearing on Reality. Because this is deeply understood, the questions aren't for the purpose of arriving at answers. This part of the process is about the *type* of questions and the way in which they are formulated. In the ajnani stage the mind booted up all kinds of concepts that had been considered valid. Gradually, concept by concept, my investigation showed me they were invalid.

Now, whatever concepts remain are recognized as being totally paradoxical. However, as long as the mind continues booting up concepts and imagery, discrimination continues. The form of discrimination happening now is very different because there is far more clarity. That is why one could say the jnani is, relatively speaking, more objective. Discrimination will, no doubt, continue until there is total objectivity. And that may or may not *happen* before the body "dies."

The greatest habit of all is the habit of intellect, which is all about "I" and "mine," which means it has everything to do with identification AS and, in my case, identification WITH.

The mind has to discriminate to the furthest extreme possible. Be it in the ajnani or jnani stage, the reversal of the process of identification can only happen when the mind trips over itself enough. In the ajnani to jnani stage, intellectual discrimination or jnana yoga isn't the only means by which the first stage of the process can end. For example, there is karma yoga, the yoga of service; bhakti yoga, the yoga of devotion and worship; and other "paths." In the next stage of the process, jnana yoga is really the only way, or at least this is my sense, because the "I" belongs to the *realm* of knowing and not-knowing. Before the "I" can subside the intellect has to be absolutely transparent. It seems that this is only possible through intense discrimination.

I guess these things aren't often talked about, but my sense is that it may help you to be clearer on the futility of trying to understand and know the Truth via the mind. It's not that you are going to voluntarily stop trying if your seeking is intense and one-pointed. There's absolutely nothing that will stop seeking once it is that way.

You just have to "get," deeper and deeper, that the mind knows nothing. As this understanding sends the mind into tighter and tighter spirals, all the other stuff you thought you understood starts falling by the wayside.

So you are destroying the mind with the mind; dissolving thinking with thoughts. It's a pastime, eh? (laughing)

An exhausting one!
Yes, it's as exhausting as any obsession. The difference is that the desire to know Self is the only healthy obsession. The stronger this obsession becomes, the less room it will leave for any other kinds of desire. Eventually it will erase all other desires.

Like any obsession, this one has the potential of "doing you in"or being your undoing. But the "you" I'm talking about is the pseudo-you of course.

So you see, seeking is really a form of suicide. (laughing)

But by the sounds of it this kind of suicide isn't exactly painless. (laughing)
No, dying to an old way of being is never painless. Then again, is believing you are a limited lump of flesh and bones painless? You just have to keep it all in perspective. Seeking is a pastime like any other, just something that's happening until it isn't anymore. Once it is fully underway it is all you can do and all you can think about in every waking moment. Then the seeking is quite out of your hands—as it always has been. It's just that once the search is all-consuming, that's the first time you really begin to "get" that *everything* happens despite you. And that's all that's necessary, that this understanding filters deeper and deeper.

Now "waking up" seems more difficult than ever! (sigh)
It is *very* difficult, and it is only in rare instances that it happens fully.

If you are sincere in your seeking then this understanding will simply make your search more one-pointed, make you more determined. Once seeking is fully underway and no longer a half-hearted passtime, to understand this can only add to your determination. At the same time this understanding will not allow you to be seduced by any pleasant phenomena that you might experience along the way. While the dream-you still figures in the dream and is still identified with, you can't rest on your laurels. You must make the mind more and more lucid.

First you have to be absolutely clear on who You are NOT. Then, if you maintain a clear perspective, you will increasingly lose interest in this dreamed figure.

Until disinterest or dispassion towards the dream-you is total, discrimination must continue. Only then is it possible to fully "wake up."

"Understanding is all."

Sri Nisargadatta Maharaj

Who am I?

9 781929 762026